SIMPLY RAW:

A guide for raw feeding your dog

Jonathan Martin

CONTENTS

1- INTRODUCTION

My own experience

The first dog I introduced to a raw-food diet was a magnificent Newfoundland, a great hairy mountain of cheerful spirit and playfulness, named Frank (who appears on the cover of this book). Frank began life on dry food – before collecting him from the breeder, when he was eight months old, I had spent weeks looking for the best possible food source. Being of a giant breed, Frank's nutritional needs were particularly specific: he needed just the right levels of calcium to ensure controlled bone growth, a high-quality source of protein, a low level of fat, and supplemental ingredients for the support of healthy joint development.

Due to these stringent nutritional demands, I had barely given raw food any consideration. I wanted a food whose nutrient levels were meticulously controlled and measured. Therefore, Frank spent his first year on a very good dry food (Orijen Large Puppy) and did very well on it. The 'biologically appropriate' diet this food provided, its extensive list of ingredients, its perfectly balanced calcium levels, and its eye-watering price point all reassured me that it was giving him a great nutritional start to life – this was also evidenced in the bouncy, joyful dog my pup was growing into.

However, as Frank approached his first birthday, I became increasingly conscious of the problem. For all the dogs I had ever known, food was more than something which should have a precise amount of calcium and an impressive list of supplementary ingredients on its packaging: food was something that gave excitement and happiness to their lives. Mealtimes should be preceded by a barrage of anticipatory and unrestrained barking with enough fervour to upset the neighbours, tails wagging dementedly and eyes brightly fixed on the bowls being prepared.

When I set down Frank's bowl of dry dog food, I had to face the reality that this mealtime excitement was utterly missing for him. He would stomp up to his bowl sombrely, dutifully, and with all the joie-de-vivre of a schoolboy settling down to his homework. After munching his way stoically through the bulk of the kibble in his bowl, he would often decide he had had enough and would plod off to find a more gratifying form of entertainment. Although the food he was getting was undoubtedly high quality, he simply wasn't finding in it any joy.

In my search for a solution I came across the raw feeding concept and began giving it serious consideration. It all looked very promising – I read about a raw diet championed by its proponents for perfectly matching a dog's biological function and temperament; I envisaged Frank's magnificent set of teeth being put to proper use: tearing up flesh rather than being made redundant by the bitty little biscuits of his dry-food diet. I still remember the very first raw food meal I gave him (minced lamb from Tesco – not, in hindsight, the best protein source to start with — mixed up with pureed vegetables) and the wonderfully rapacious way he received it. Raw feeding allowed me to give a natural, healthy, and — no less important — enjoyable diet that cannot be matched by commercial foods bought off the shelf.

The learning journey from that first meal to where I am now has been a long and useful one; my findings from it are what I offer in this book. Because Frank was the first dog I introduced this diet to, and because with him I had my most revelatory and educational raw-food experiences, he will be making a few appearances with some of his personal reflections.

2- RAW FEEDING: THE PROS AND CONS

ADVANTAGES:

1) Quality

The prime advantage of raw feeding has to be the uncompromised nutritional quality provided by this diet. Dogs need meat, and this is what they get when you raw feed.

To understand the advantages of raw feeding over a commercial diet, you might take a look at the 'composition' section of the nutritional information on the food you currently give to your dog. Some sort of meat should be the first listed ingredient; however, very low-quality foods will have a cereal as the first listed. This means that the actual meat content of the food is very low indeed, and it is largely bulked out by corn, wheat, or some other cereal grain.

The trouble with this is that dogs do not have the biological design to digest cereals. Dogs are carnivores, not herbivores. Although it's great for pet food companies to pad out their food with cheap cereal, it is not beneficial for your dog if it forms more of the diet than meat. In fact, due to the canine digestive system being poorly designed to cope with low-quality cereals, it can be harmful. Allergic reactions and all manner of digestive difficulties can result from too much cereal in the food. If, for example, your dog's guts have a tendency to 'explode', this is likely due to cereal content and is a great reason to move to raw feeding, or at the very least a better-quality commercial food.

Going back to the ingredients list on your current pet food – you might see the phrase 'animal derivatives'. This is a low-quality meat source and is another indicator of lacklustre dog food. 'Animal derivatives' means the bits of the animal that couldn't be used for more profitable means, such as human consumption; this includes beaks, feet, feathers, hooves...generally all the bits you wouldn't want to find on your dinner plate. Whilst these aren't necessarily harmful to your dog (they do, as we'll see later, have their place in a raw-food diet), they are obviously not the most nutritious parts of the animal and feeding a diet which largely comprises of such derivatives will be detrimental.

Better quality foods will name a proper meat source with a percentage, for example 'chicken (20%)'. This means that 20% of the can, pouch, or whatever contains actual, proper chicken. The higher the percentage, the better. Decent food will have at least 60% meat. However, these foods can still be bulked out by cereals, and the true nature of the meat source can be debatable. If the ingredients list says 'dried meat', this means the meat has been processed for preservative purposes and has lost much of its nutritional integrity. The best foods will say 'fresh meat'; however, even here the meat can be bulked out with water to keep the company's cost down.

Most foods available in the supermarket are of the cereal-rich, 'animal derivative' variety – though pricier and better foods are becoming more frequently stocked. However, when you buy a commercial food you can never be sure of what exact quality of meat your dog is receiving, nor what sort of preservative processes may have compromised the meat's nutritional integrity before it lands in your dog's dinner bowl. Of course, sourcing your own raw food circumvents these problems.

One would naturally think that a higher quality, natural meat would come at a higher financial outlay – thankfully, this need not be the case. Whilst you will have to be prepared to spend more than the cost of cheap supermarket foods, you won't have to spend more than a decent-quality commercial food. A later section of this guide will go into sourcing food in detail.

2) Fun

The sheer enjoyment value contained in a raw food diet is, I believe, one of its greatest assets. There's something about seeing a dog using his teeth in the way nature intended which is immensely gratifying. A raw food diet puts dogs' teeth and jaws to proper use, making mealtimes more enjoyable and satisfying.

Moreover, the variety of a raw food diet helps to keep it interesting. Once you have learned about what to feed, you will realise that raw feeding does not involve putting down the same bowl of food, day in day out, as happens with a commercial diet. If you have one of those dogs who seems to lose interest in his food after a few days because he wants something different, then raw feeding provides an ideal solution.

Raw feeding can be great fun for owners, as well as dogs. I like shopping around for unusual new meats to feed, and it's great to peruse the reduced-items sections in supermarkets to find interesting, often high-quality cuts of meat at bargain prices.

3) Control

One of the great strengths of a raw-food diet is its versatility, and the control it offers you over meeting the specific nutritional needs of your dog. For example, if you have an older dog who puts on weight easily, you can choose to feed meats with lower fat content. Or, you might have a dog with delicate joints – you can use food rich in glucosamine, chondroitin, and other ingredients which promote joint support. Perhaps you have a dog with itchy skin or dry coat; again, you can tailor your dog's diet to contain foods which well help with these issues. The chapter 'TAILORING DIET' will show you what sorts of food can help with common health problems. Once you have some knowledge, you can control your dog's diet to make it the best for him.

4) Health

The main reason for choosing a raw-food diet is to give your dog the best possible source of nutrition, and the benefits generally become readily apparent a couple of months after making the switch. You are likely to see:

- Better condition in your dog's coat.
- Less itching.
- A dog who was quite smelly will become noticeably less so.
- Bright, clear eyes.
- An energetic, cheerful dog.

Commercial foods contain preservatives and chemicals which act as toxins to your dog's body. Often, switching to a raw-food diet results in a period of detox – the built up chemicals will be purged from your dog's system. Some of this will occur through the skin, so you might notice your dog smells a bit more at first – but this will soon disappear.

The poo from a raw-fed dog is smaller than a commercially fed dog's. This is because there are fewer waste materials in the meat you will be feeding, less indigestible matter to be excreted. Poo also won't smell nearly half as much as when it was fuelled by commercial food. If it's not picked up, the poo will turn to a whitish powder after a couple of days and be blown away by the wind.

Analogies are often made between cheap commercial dog foods and human 'fast food'. A dog kept on a commercial diet will experience the same sort of health deficits as a human sustained by 'drive-thru' burgers. Switching to raw food detoxifies your dog and opens up a much healthier future.

DISADVANTAGES:

1) Practicalities

In terms of sheer convenience for the owner, a raw-food diet can't match up to commercial food.

Firstly, obtaining the food is not quite so simple as loading some cans or sacks into your shopping trolley. However, it need not be as difficult as you might think. See the chapter 'WHERE TO GET RAW FOOD'.

Secondly, the preparation is a bit more involved and time consuming than with commercial food, and can be a bit messier.

Finally, storage can be an issue. Because the most cost-effective approach to raw feeding is buying frozen food in bulk, you'll need a good bit of freezer space to store it. When I first started, I bought a second-hand chest freezer (about the size of a standard fridge) for £25 and this gave me plenty of room along with my fridge-freezer unit.

2) Mess and hygiene

Yes, you'll be handling things such as raw chicken and slicing up odd bits of animals. When your dog's really getting stuck into his raw grub, little bits of raw meat will be splashing out of the bowl and onto your kitchen floor. You'll need to do quite a bit of cleaning up after preparing and feeding the raw food, in the interests of hygiene.

3) Knowledge

Personally, I don't see this as a disadvantage – but I can understand how some might find the learning investment you need to make in order to really effectively feed a raw diet inconvenient. You'll need to learn what food to give your dog, and how to feed it (but the fact you're reading this book shows you don't mind doing this!). You'll also need to pay close attention to how your dog responds to the diet – particularly, but not exclusively, in the early stages. This means being sensitive to any changes in health/condition/energy, etc., and responding by adjusting diet accordingly. You'll also need to monitor closely what comes out of your dog's rear end and make appropriate dietary changes (if the poo is consistently too hard or too soft, for example).

4) Safety

There's no getting away from the fact that you will be feeding raw meat which can contain bacteria such as salmonella. Whilst many of these bacteria do not pose a risk to your dog (see 'FAQS'), they do to humans. Bacteria is shed in faeces, and will therefore be present when your dog goes to the toilet in the garden; bits of faecal matter may be transferred from your dog onto your household carpets and furniture, etc. Good hygiene and cleanliness obviously helps a great deal here, and in my raw-feeding experience I have never suffered any illness due to bacteria from my dog's meat. However, if there are any members of your household in a high-risk category (infants, elderly people, pregnant women) you might want to be a bit warier about beginning a raw diet.

Overall, care and planning can circumvent the above disadvantages, and you are likely to find the advantages make a few inconveniences very much worthwhile.

3- THE THEORY OF RAW FEEDING

Although you by no means need any sort of background or expertise in veterinary science in order to start a raw-food diet, a basic grasp of current concepts can help you understand what makes an effective diet.

There are two main schools of current raw-food theory. These are known as:

1) The 'prey-model' diet
2) The 'BARF' diet.

Both these schools of thought work along the lines of giving the dog a diet which matches, as closely as possible, what the dog's internal systems are naturally designed to receive. Both diets aim to replicate what dogs would eat in the wild.

Some raw feeders see more merit in the prey-model diet, others stick to BARF concepts. You might prefer to take ideas from both – that is what I do. Let's take a closer look at each one.

PREY MODEL

The prey-model diet involves feeding an entire animal to the dog. The idea behind this is that in the wild, dogs would naturally consume every bit of their prey – bones, organs, flesh, feathers, hair, feet, beaks, etc. – and so this is what we should be feeding them to make sure they get all the nutrition of their natural diet.

Where feeding whole prey is not practical or possible, the raw feeder may use the following ratio to imitate a whole prey diet:

80% muscle meat
10% organs (5% being liver)
10% bone.

However, one of the big benefits of the prey-model diet is the enjoyment for your dog – tearing up whole animals with his teeth releases endorphins; gnawing on bones cleans teeth. Therefore, minced meats and minced bone are eschewed in favour of big cuts of meat and chunky, meaty bones.

The idea of tossing a chicken/fish/rabbit etc. to our dogs and letting them get on with it as nature intended is appealing – however, I have found that it normally doesn't go quite to plan. Dogs don't always know what to do with a whole animal. Frank would quite enjoy wandering about with a salmon clutched in his mouth, and would find a nice spot in the garden to bury it, but the thought of actually eating the thing never seemed to occur to him.

I have had much more success following the ratio, using big cuts of meat wherever possible so those teeth and jaws get some good exercise, and feeding a wide variety of meat, bone and offal. Chicken carcasses are excellent as part of a prey-model diet – they are appealing, dogs seem to know they are supposed to eat them, they are big and satisfying to chow down on, and are a good source of meat and bone. Salmon heads also work well – they are more accessible to the dog than a whole fish, but still contain unusual bits (eyes, brains, etc.) that make up a well-rounded, complete diet.

Ultimately, we want our dogs to get a wide range of nutrition in their diet. This means not just feeding cuts of meat, but also all the other bits of animals (even pelt/feathers) so the dog gets full nutritional benefit. So you might well try offering a whole animal, but don't be surprised if you need to find a way of making it more accessible to your dog by feeding meat, organs and bones separately.

BARF

'BARF' is an acronym for 'biologically appropriate raw food', or 'bones and raw food'. Similar to the prey-model diet, BARF is designed to imitate what nature intended our dogs to eat. There are two big differences between BARF and prey-model:

1) BARF doesn't place the same importance on feeding whole animals as the prey-model diet does. A BARF feeder will happily feed minced meat.
2) Whereas the prey-model feeder will only feed animals, a BARF feeder will supplement with fruit, vegetables, and anything else that might bring nutritional benefit.

It might seem an odd idea, to feed your dog fruits and vegetables. One look at a dog's teeth is enough to conclude that they certainly aren't herbivores. So why do BARF feeders do it? Well, of course there are the good nutrients provided by fruit and veg, but remember that our aim is to imitate the natural diet of a dog. When a wild dog consumes a prey, it eats the prey's stomach and the stomach's contents, which could often include fruit, vegetable and grains.

Yes – a BARF feeder may decide to feed grain. But a healthy grain, which is a supplementary ingredient and a small proportion of the total diet – so very different to the unhealthy, processed grain which bulks out commercial dog food and leads to so many digestive issues.

A BARF diet involves a bit more complexity in preparation than the prey model, because it encourages the use of an enormous range of ingredients and supplements. Consequently, you can tailor the diet really quite precisely to your dog's particular needs.

PREY-MODEL OR BARF?

You will likely want to enjoy experimenting with both concepts to find out what works best for you and your dog. Perhaps you know a local gamekeeper who can provide you with whole animals which your dog delights in devouring, or perhaps you want more precise control over your dog's nutritional intake.

I have always mixed prey-model and BARF concepts. For example, one of my dogs' meals will be minced meat and bone with a range of fruit and/or vegetables mixed into it. A later meal (in the same day) will perhaps consist of meaty lamb rib bones, or a chicken carcass, or turkey neck, or maybe a whole fish. This sort of diet incorporates both the BARF and prey-model benefits. Later chapters will go into more detail about what exactly you could feed, but for now let's take a look at an example menu to see more precisely how BARF and prey-model elements can work together.

EXAMPLE MENU

Dogs of different sizes and energy levels need different quantities and different types of food, and diets can be tailored to meet dogs' individual needs. But to give an example of a complete raw-food diet, I will outline here what I fed my 60kg Newfoundland Frank each day.

Don't worry too much at this stage about each ingredient – subsequent chapters will explain in detail the benefits of particular ingredients.

BREAKFAST:
Whole fish (sardines or a kipper were popular with Frank)
50-100g cooked brown rice. Or, once or twice a week, the same quantity of rolled porridge oats soaked overnight in water and yoghurt.
1 tablespoon natural goats' yoghurt
1 raw egg with shell (twice a week)
1 teaspoon kelp powder
1 – 2 teaspoons tinned pumpkin (twice a week).
All the above mashed up and mixed together.

EARLY EVENING MEAL (about 4pm):
500g minced meat with ground bone (10%). Chicken, turkey, lamb, beef, or sometimes venison – alternating each day.
1 – 2 tablespoons pureed vegetables and/or fruit, lightly cooked. I use a wide range of fruit and veg, keeping it varied

each meal (see 'FEEDING VEGETABLES AND FRUITS' for more on the types of fruit and vegetables you can include).

1-2 teaspoons of coconut oil, or salmon oil, or flaxseed oil.

To help maintain Frank's healthy joints, I would also add 500mg of ester-c and about ½ a teaspoon of Riaflex (a supplement to support joints).

LATE EVENING MEAL (about 10pm):

This is where things get more interesting and varied. What I fed Frank at this meal would change each day, so I will take you through a typical week:

Monday: 500g big beef chunks and some meaty lamb ribs.

Tuesday: 500g liver followed by a few duck feet and a beef trachea (yes – that's a cow's windpipe; Frank loved them!).

Wednesday: A chicken carcass and about 400g diced heart.

Thursday: 500g green tripe and a whole fish (maybe a kipper, or a few sardines, or a small trout (although Frank went off these).

Friday: a whole duck (depending on Franks mood, the whole thing would go down or he would just tear out the flesh and eat that. For some reason, duck was the only whole-prey food he would take, apart from fish).

Saturday: 500g beef or lamb chunks and a meaty lamb leg bone.

Sunday: whole rabbit (these were skinned and sometimes gutted, though I would get them with innards whenever possible. Frank wouldn't eat them whole, so I would chop them up).

By no means would I follow this menu religiously, but it shows the sort of range of foods Frank would get.

Notice how the early evening meal provides the BARF element, where I give the additional supplements and ingredients mixed into the minced meat, and the later evening meal is more of the prey-model concept, with whole foods, or large cuts.

I would always aim to hit the golden ratio: 10% bone, 10% offal, and the rest meat.

FASTING

Some raw feeders choose to incorporate a weekly fast day, because it mimics the dog's natural behaviour. I would judge a need for a fast day by Frank's appetite – sometimes he would appear not to be very hungry, and sometimes his poo would be quite yellowish, indicating a need for his digestive system to have a break. A diet which includes a fast day needs to have the volume of food increased accordingly on non-fasting days.

4- FAQS

These are some of the questions I had when I first began thinking about raw feeding, and which many other people have too.

Raw chicken? Really? What about salmonella?!

It's an undeniably stomach-churning thought, and it will feel somewhat uncomfortable when you first start raw feeding, but the simple fact is that dogs' internal systems are very different to ours. They have shorter intestines, which do not allow certain bacteria, including salmonella, to trouble them in the same way is it does for us humans.

So, yes, it is safe to feed raw chicken, and raw food in general. However, there are some precautionary steps with certain foods you need to take in order to protect your dog from bacteria which can harm him. For example, any fish you give should have been frozen for at least a week before you offer it, as this kills off a harmful bacteria harboured by fish. See the chapter 'FEEDING MEAT' for more details.

What about bones? Surely it must be dangerous to allow a dog to eat a bone!

Again, dogs' digestive systems are simply better able to cope with bone than humans' are. In all my raw feeding experience, I have never encountered a problem caused by feeding bone, and I don't know of anyone who has!

However, you do need to be careful about what type of bone you feed (see the chapter 'FEEDING BONES') and you must always abide by the golden rule: **never feed cooked bones**.

Cooked bones are hard and brittle; if they splinter when eaten, the shards can do damage to your dog's internals. Raw bones – the right sort – are soft and digestible, as well as being healthy and fun to eat.

How do I know I am feeding my dog the right food and the right variety?

This is one of the trickier aspects with raw feeding. Achieving a balanced diet which supplies your dog with all his nutritional needs is not straightforward, and you need to educate yourself on the right way to go about it – you've already made a great start by deciding to read this guide!

Treat raw feeding as an educational experience; keep reading about it and keep looking for a good variety of food you can give to your dog.

Problems caused by nutritional insufficiencies and imbalances are sometimes easily identifiable – you will, for example, become an expert at 'reading' your dog's poo. However, often these problems don't manifest for months or even years, so it is important to learn as much as you can about how to feed an effective diet. Keep reading!

Will raw feeding change my dog's behaviour?

I've often wondered, especially after tossing my dog a chicken carcass or whole rabbit to devour, whether he might start eyeing up other people's pets hungrily having been given a taste for meat in its natural form.   Happily, the only behaviour changes I can report from my experience are those brought about by the increased healthiness, energy and vivaciousness that a really good and nutritious raw diet provides.

My vet says raw feeding is not a good idea. Why do people do it if the professionals advise against it?

Sometimes people are warned off raw feeding by their vets. My own vet is all for a raw diet, and gives it to her own dog (and cat). I think it is important to listen very carefully to your vet's concerns – especially if they are advising you against a raw diet due to your dog's specific condition or needs.
        One can only speak from experience. The dogs I have fed raw food have never had any diet-related problem. A good way to put your mind at ease is to research the experience of other raw feeders, for which the internet is a marvellous resource.

It all seems very complicated and I don't think I can do it.

Yes – it can become complex (look at all the different ingredients in my 'example menu' above) – but not in a way that has to confuse you, or your dog. As you'll see, you start in a very simple way and build up a diet that works for your dog. From there, you may tailor the diet as intricately as you wish. It is not hard to feed a safe, healthy diet, provided you are willing to undergo a little learning. The learning experience can be great fun for you and your dog! Above all, if it's not working out, you don't have to stick to it. But there is little reason not to give it a shot.

5- GOLDEN RULES

Raw feeding is a safe, healthy and enjoyable way to feed your dog – provided you stick to the following 'rules'. If you absorb anything at all from this book, let it be this chapter!

1) Never feed cooked bones.

Cooked bones are hard and brittle; splintered shards will damage a dog's intestines in a way that raw bones won't.

2) 80% muscle meat – 10% bone – 10% offal.

You might start raw feeding and find that your dog loves chunks of raw chicken breast – great, but don't go on to only feed chucks of raw chicken breast. An effective diet needs to be varied. The above ratio is a good backbone for an effective diet; following chapters will show you in more detail how to offer good and nutritious variety.

3) Check before feeding.

One of the great joys of raw feeding is the tremendous range of food you can give to your dog; it is great fun looking for new, adventurous ingredients. However, there are some foods which are harmful to canines that might be fine for humans, so make sure you research any type of meat, fruit, vegetable etc. before offering it to your dog.

4) Eyes open.

For a dog who is used to hoovering up dry dog food, the experience of tearing into proper meat can take a bit of getting used to (though he will find it delightful!). So, always supervise your dog when he's eating, but especially when first starting the raw diet. Make sure he is tearing/chewing it sufficiently. Make sure he isn't attempting to gulp down big bits of meat. This can cause bad digestive problems, and if you're very unlucky could trigger bloat.

Same goes for feeding bones: make sure your dog isn't swallowing big bits of bone; he should be gnawing and crunching them down into digestible bits. If in doubt, remove the food from the dog (see 'FEEDING BONES' for more advice).

Keep a close eye on how your dog responds to the new diet. Some behavioural changes are to be expected (see chapter 10) but don't hesitate to contact a vet if anything seems to be going amiss.

5) Water.

As always, make sure your dog has open access to fresh water.

If your dog is a breed susceptible to bloat (such as large breeds), don't offer water immediately before or after feeding.

6- WHERE TO GET RAW FOOD

Sourcing your dog's raw food easily and cheaply can be one of the biggest obstacles to a successful raw-food diet. You'll likely need a bit of determination here; raw feeding is not yet a common enough practice to make raw meat for dogs immediately straightforward to procure – but doing a bit of research and hunting about should allow you to find a few ways of obtaining it economically. This chapter gives my suggestions for where you can look.

1)   Specialist raw-food merchants.

These are becoming more widespread and accessible as raw-food diets become more popular. Specialist raw-food suppliers sell all the different types of meats and supplements you will need, and they cater exclusively to pets – which means they are much cheaper to buy than human-grade meats.

Usually, these meats will be sourced from an abattoir, but they won't have undergone the processing that makes them suitable for human consumption. But they are perfectly fine for your dog.

If you are lucky, you will find one of these merchants near where you live. But if not, many of these companies will deliver. You can put in an order on their websites, or via a phone call. However, some companies have quite a large minimum order for deliveries, so you will need to buy in bulk. If you don't have enough freezer space, consider buying a cheap second-hand freezer; they can be found for very reasonable prices.

I am lucky enough to live just a couple of minutes away from Bulmer Pet Foods, where I go to stock up on most of the raw food I need. Bulmer sell me all variety of ground meats (a crate of 30 x 1lb packs costs between £14-£16, depending on the type of meat). They also supply green tripe, chunks of beef, liver, necks, trachea, heart, chicken carcasses, feet, heads, fish, among many others. They also sell supplements such as kelp powder, coconut oil, salmon oil, etc. – all for very good prices.

This is certainly the sort of place you want to find, whether it's locally or a company who can deliver to you.

Here are some websites to look at, but there are many other companies. Check on the internet to see if you can find a supplier near you. Try running a search for 'raw food for dogs', or something similar. Include your postcode or use the 'maps' search to help find any merchants in your area.

Bulmer Pet Food
www.bulmerdogfood.co.uk

Raw Pet Supplies
www.rawpetsupplies.co.uk

Raw To Go
www.rawtogo.co.uk

DAF Petfoods
www.daf-petfood.co.uk

Manifold Valley Meats
www.manifoldvalleymeats.co.uk

Paleo Ridge Raw (good for whole-prey foods; sells more unusual items including buffalo, zebra and ostrich meat!) www.paleoridgeraw.uk

2) The supermarket.

The very first raw meal I gave to my dog was a packet of lamb mince from Tesco; it cost me about £2.50. Frank loved it.

Now, I never buy full-price meat from supermarkets for two reasons: firstly, it is not the most economical way to source your raw food; secondly, the meat in supermarkets is treated in a way that makes it hygienic and appealing to humans, but not necessarily to dogs. Most of my raw food comes from specialist merchants (see above). It's still perfectly good meat, but seems to have a more exciting smell for dogs, and is much cheaper than supermarket meat.

However, supermarkets have these wonderful 'reduced items' sections which often offer some good bargain-priced meat.

Morrisons is particularly good as they sell the 'who-would-eat-that?' items such as bones, heart, pigs' trotters, etc. which make great components of a raw-food diet.

You certainly can't rely on a supermarket as your sole source of raw products, though. Apart from the amount of money it would cost, there's also the problem that some of the more unusual ingredients aren't available in the supermarket. The only tripe, for example, you can buy off the shelf is bleached (to make it more appealing to human consumers), not the natural green tripe which is so good for your dog. Bleached tripe has undergone processing which removes many of the wonderful nutritional properties found in natural green tripe.

3) Butchers

Butchers can be a good source for whole-prey food; they can often provide you with whole animals – sometimes skinned and gutted, but if you're lucky ones which are completely intact. You can also get larger cuts of meat here, which your dog will enjoy tearing up.

Unfortunately, butchers do tend to be expensive. A good approach is to visit your local butchers and explain that you are looking for food for your dog. Your butcher might be able to supply you with cheap offcuts.

I have had mixed success with this approach. Some butchers said that they are unable to sell offcuts at discounted prices due to legislation, whereas others have been happy to do so. A wonderful local butchers I have recently started using sells bags of frozen dog food, 500g in weight, for fifty pence. It consists of meat, offal, heart and lung, and goes down very well.

All butchers will sell raw bones which can be very helpful as uncooked bones can be tricky to find (pet shops all seem to sell just cooked bones, which should not be fed to a dog).

4) Ethnic meat markets/butchers

If you have any of these in your area, you can often find more exotic cuts of meat which may well be worth trying in your dog's diet.

5) Abattoirs

Check to see if you've got any abattoirs in your area and give them a call. It would help if you have an idea of the sorts of meats you are hoping the abattoir can provide before calling, so draw up a list. Some may be reluctant or unable to deal with individuals, but it can't hurt to try.

6) Pet shops

As raw feeding becomes a more popular practice, more and more pet shops are selling supplies. You will probably be able to find packets of frozen raw food (such as beef chunks, tripe, heart etc.) in your local pet shop. You will also find 'complete' raw meals, which are packs of minced meat with supplements mixed in. All this tends to be more expensive than from other sources, but it is worth having a look.

You won't have much luck buying bones from pet shops. I haven't yet found a pet shop which sells raw bone; they only sell cooked bones which we do not want to give to our dogs.

7) Health-food shops

You won't find much in the way of raw meat and bones here, but health-food shops can be useful for some of the other supplements that you may wish to add to your dog's diet, such as kelp, Ester-c, etc.

8) Ask about

Put the word out among your friends and family that you are starting a raw diet; you might find someone can help out. My brother has connections with a local gamekeeper, and managed to hook me up with a supply of venison cuts. I used to know the head chef at the local pub who could occasionally send unwanted cuts my way. You might be surprised at what generous offers you receive.

7- STORING AND DEFROSTING MEAT

As the meat eaters among us will know, meat which has been frozen doesn't taste quite so good, or have the same tenderness, as fresh meat. But your dog isn't likely to mind, and freezing meat won't cause it to lose its nutrition – in fact, it can be a good way to preserve nutrients.

Some human-grade meat is processed before being frozen in a way that can cause a bit of nutritional detriment, which could be a good reason to avoid purchasing food from the frozen sections in supermarkets.

So, you can freeze all your dog's meat (including bones and offal) without worrying about it losing any nutritional quality. Fruit and vegetables, however, are best used fresh. Meat can be kept in the freezer for about four months, though some types of meat can be kept for longer.

Fish must be frozen for at least a week before feeding it so as to kill of parasites that may be present in raw fish. You might want to treat pork in the same way if you are concerned about the slight risk of Trichinella Spiralis. Other meats are fine to feed fresh.

Meat needs to be defrosted in the right way to minimise the amount of bacteria that can grow on it while it is defrosting. The safest way to defrost is in the fridge because the low temperatures prevent bacteria forming on the meat. This is the only safe way to defrost large cuts of meat. Allow 4-5 hours of defrosting time for each 500g of meat.

Once defrosted, poultry, fish and ground meat can be stored in a refrigerator for 1-2 days safely. Beef, pork and lamb (not ground) can be stored for 3-5 days.

It is best not to defrost meat in the microwave – if the meat has any bone content, this can result in hardening of the bone that may make it dangerous for your dog to consume. We must never feed bones that have been cooked or partially cooked.

However, there is a quicker way to defrost small bits of meat. If you are feeding thin steaks or small chunks, you can defrost them in warm water. Feed as soon as it is defrosted.

This is safe because with thin meat, the interior defrosts at the same time (more or less) as the exterior. It is not safe for large bits of meat because the exterior would defrost first and bacteria would start forming on the exterior while the interior is still in the process of thawing.

For the same reason, meat should not be defrosted at room temperature. There is too much discrepancy between the time the exterior of the meat defrosts and the time the interior defrosts, which allows bacteria to form on the exterior before the meat is fully thawed.

Meat is only safe to refreeze after thawing if it was thawed in a refrigerator.

Thought from Frank:

Sometimes it's nice to eat food when it's still frozen, or partly defrosted. I'm particularly fond of frozen sardines, though I wouldn't want to try and work my way into a big hard bit of frozen meat or bone.

8- USEFUL EQUIPMENT FOR RAW FEEDERS

Don't worry – you're not going to have to go out and spend lots of money on expensive equipment to start raw feeding. Most equipment that might useful is probably already in your kitchen.

SCALES
Useful for making sure you are feeding the right quantities of meat.

FOOD PROCESSOR
This is essential for feeding fruits and vegetables (see chapter 15) which must be pureed to make them digestible for your dog. A good quality blender is best, because the more broken down the puree is, the more efficiently it will be digested.

A GOOD SHARP KNIFE
For slicing up all sorts of different types of meat. Things like tripe can be really tough to cut, so a sharp knife will help.

SMALL PLASTIC BAGS
I have found these invaluable in my raw-feeding experience for storing different cuts of meat in the freezer and for

defrosting small bits of meat in warm water. Supermarkets sell cheap rolls of small bin-liners – the ones I buy come in rolls of 100 for £1.

STICKY LABELS/MARKER PENS
If you've got a freezer full of different types of meat and offal you might find it useful to have some sort of labelling system to keep track of what's what, when it was frozen, etc.

SPOONS
Teaspoons for measuring out quantities of supplements, wooden spoons for mixing meat and fruit/vegetable blends together.

9- HOW TO START

The most important point about starting a raw-food diet is to keep it simple. The first couple of weeks should consist of very straightforward meals with a single protein source.

Don't worry about trying to give a varied, balanced diet right from the outset – we want a simple, smooth start which gets your dog comfortably onto raw food. Balance and variety can come with time; there is no rush.

Chicken is a good meat to begin with – it's simple, easily digestible, and very appetising. It is a good idea to feed meat with bone for the first few meals; the calcium content helps to firm up poo.

Don't panic about feeding your dog bone – this is what nature intends him to eat! Provided you choose the right sort of meat and bone for your dog, his first meals should be a really enjoyable experience.

For small dogs, chicken wings or necks are a good choice. Chicken legs, breast quarters or carcasses are better for medium to large dogs. If you feed small portions, such as chicken wings, to a large dog there is a risk he will gulp it down without crunching it up properly.

Smaller dogs such as terriers should be fine with wings or necks. Anything above about 15kgs would be better off with legs or breast quarters.

To start with, you should aim to feed about 2% of your dog's weight each day (assuming your dog is an adult). This can be split over more than one meal if that is what your dog is used to having.

When we change our dogs' commercial food, we are always advised to make a gradual transition – mixing increasingly large proportions of the new food with the old food over the course of a couple of weeks. There is no need to do this when starting a raw diet. You can make a clean cut. Simply stop feeding the old food and start with the raw. Many people start a raw diet because they want something healthier for their dog than the commercial food he's been on; it's best just to stop feeding that horrible commercial food as soon as possible.

You may want to fast your dog for a day to clean out his digestive system before starting the new food; this might help to ease the transition. I have never felt the need to do this, and have never had a problem with an immediate switch. However, if your dog is susceptible to stomach upsets when eating a different food to what he is used to, this might be worth doing.

Most likely, your dog will be thrilled to find a nice meal of raw chicken in his bowl and really enjoy his first meal. Some dogs, however, might be taken aback by the new food and not know what they are expected to do with it. If your dog turns his nose up at the first raw meal, there are a few things you can do:

1) Remove the meal and don't offer anything else. When his next meal time comes around, give him a fresh offering of raw chicken. This might need to be

repeated several times before your dog gets the idea that he is supposed to eat this new food. Don't worry; he won't starve himself. Once he is hungry enough, he will dig in and most likely get the taste for it once he's started.

2) You could make the food more tempting my sprinkling a bit of cheese on the top, or by pouring a low-salt chicken or beef broth over it.

3) You could try adding a little of your dog's old food with the raw chicken. This will encourage him to view the meal with less suspicion, and he'll get the taste for the chicken after a few bites. There should be no need to continue mixing for future meals.

4) Although it is recommended to start with bone-in chicken, if your dog isn't taking to this you could try boneless chicken instead. Gently heating the chicken can make it smellier and therefore more appetising; this is likely to encourage a reticent dog. It should only be lightly heated, just enough to awaken the smell – not cooked through. Make sure it isn't hot when you offer it to your dog. A danger of this approach is that it can lead to 'spoiling' your dog – he might not eat any raw meat in the future unless it has been heated. So it can be good for encouraging your dog to take the first step, but don't do it beyond the first meal. Any meat with bone in it should not be heated, as it can make the bones brittle and risks doing damage to your dog's insides.

5) You could try a different meat – it may simply be that chicken is not appealing to him. Beef, pork, turkey and lamb are fine to try (although red meats are richer and more likely to upset the stomach of a raw-food newcomer). If you try one of these meats, don't feed it with bones. Chicken bones are the softest and your dog's first bone meals should be chicken.

Some dogs can be stubborn, particularly if they have become addicted to the artificially improved taste of cheap commercial foods. It's like convincing a kid who loves Big Macs to eat vegetables instead. Persevere – your dog's health is worth it!

Keep feeding the same simple meal of bone-in chicken for the first week or two. Giving a variety of different meats too soon can lead to diarrhoea, so give his digestive system time to adapt.

Your dog's poo should stay reasonably firm thanks to the high calcium of the first few meals. You can then start offering more muscle meat, reducing the overall bone content toward 10% of the total diet. Boneless chicken meat, gizzards or heart meat can be introduced.

After a couple of weeks on chicken, introduce a different protein source along with the chicken such as beef, lamb, turkey or pork. You can feed chicken one day and a different meat the next day. Mixing meats in the same meal is a bit more likely to cause stomach upsets.

Keep feeding your bone-in chicken meat, too, but continue reducing it toward the 10% overall bone content.

Leave a week between the introduction of new protein sources. A schedule might look like this:

Week 1: bone-in chicken.
Week 2: bone-in and boneless chicken.
Week 3: chicken and beef.
Week 4: chicken, beef, lamb.
Week 5: chicken, beef, lamb, turkey.
Week 6: chicken, beef, lamb, fish.
Week 7: beef, turkey, lamb, liver (at this point you should be able to start mixing up the variety without problem).

That is not necessarily the order in which you should introduce new proteins – for example, you might prefer to introduce lamb in week 3 instead of beef – but it shows the idea of leaving a week before introducing a new protein source.

Keep feeding bones – you could introduce lamb with a lamb neck or rib meal, for example.

Wait until about week 7 or 8 before you start giving offal – it is richer, and more likely to stir up stomach trouble for a dog new to raw food.

POO CHECK

You will want to keep a close eye on your dog's poo, especially when first starting the raw diet.

Soft, quite runny poo is to be expected at first. If it's really soft and runny, this might be because you haven't yet started including bones, so try the wings/back/breast bones.

With commercial diets, we are advised to feed a bland meal of rich and boiled chicken or white fish to alleviate very runny stool. This is not necessary on a raw diet;

a better approach is to allow a day of fasting and then keep feeding the bone-in chicken. We want the high calcium content top firm up stool.

If it's diarrhoea, then there's a problem. Normally, diarrhoea occurs when a raw feeder has given too much too soon – too rich a meat, or offal, or a mix of meats. If you have followed the advice above, your dog should not suffer diarrhoea. If it does happen, you should fast your dog for a day, and then offer bone-in chicken. Diarrhoea which persists needs swift veterinary consultation.

There are a couple of supplements you can add to help your dog's digestion, and which can help keep poo nice and firm:

Tinned pumpkin is a great source of natural dietary fibre and can work miracles for a dog suffering with loose stools. This must be pure pumpkin, not a pie mix. In Britain, tinned pumpkin is available from large Tesco supermarkets and Waitrose – or you can order it online.

A good probiotic can also aid digestion. Natural goat's yoghurt is good, and available in larger supermarkets; low-fat or fat-free natural Greek yoghurt can also be used.

Just a teaspoon of pumpkin or yoghurt for smaller dogs, two teaspoons for medium dogs (15-35kgs) and a heaped tablespoon for larger dogs with each meal should be enough to help.

HAVE FUN

A raw diet is a much more kinaesthetic, active eating process than a commercial diet and it's good to let your dog enjoy this aspect of it where possible. He will discover that his food is now 'portable' – big cuts of meat and raw meaty bones can be carried off to wherever he might like to eat them.

If he wants to take his food outside into the garden, why not let him? Provided you don't spray any sort of pesticides, herbicides or other chemicals on your lawn, it won't matter if his food gets a bit of grass or mud on it.

You could even hide some of his food outside so he gets the enjoyment of 'hunting' it. When I fed Frank duck feet I would go to the garden door and launch them into various spots around the garden; he'd have a lovely time sniffing them out. Often, a few minutes later he would return to the kitchen with a duck foot dangling out of his mouth and a look on his face that said: 'chase me'. He absolutely loved being chased while he had food in his mouth. I had to be a bit careful, because exercise around eating time can increase the risk of bloat for dogs who are prone to the condition. But it was one way that food became much more entertaining for Frank when he started his raw diet.

You will likely see that your dog doesn't necessarily want to eat food from his bowl (unless it is minced meat, or something that has to be contained in a bowl), so make it clear from the outset where it is okay and where it is not okay for him to enjoy his meat.

Thought from Frank:

For some reason, my owner got upset when I did my very best to bury a salmon head in his sofa. After he managed to make the rules a bit clearer, I simply took my food out to the garden and enjoyed it in a private corner.

10-   WHAT YOU MIGHT OBSERVE WHEN STARTING A RAW DIET

DETOX

Once he's underway on his raw diet, your dog will likely start a detoxification process. This is when all those unnatural preservatives and other chemicals in commercial food are purged from his system. Your dog might start to smell – this is because of the purging. It's a good sign, and don't worry, it won't last. You might also observe a bit of discharge around the eye, and maybe some dandruff – again, all temporary. This detoxification can also cause some of the soft poo which is common when first starting a raw-food diet.

VOMITING

Whenever you start your dog on a new diet, there is a chance he will experience 'vomiting' – although it may not actually be vomiting.

If, within an hour or so of being eaten, your dog's meal comes back out of his mouth and lands on your carpet, this is probably not vomiting but regurgitation. Take a close look at it – if the food seems undigested, then this is regurgitation and is not necessarily a cause for concern.

Dogs will regurgitate food when the stomach can't quite cope with digesting it in the form it was received; it allows the dog to have another chew, which breaks it down more, and makes digestion easier.

This can occur when starting a raw diet because it is a new, different food and your dog's stomach needs time to adjust to it.

If your dog is happy to have another go at eating the regurgitated food, you should let him. This might seem unpleasant, and our instinct is to clear away the regurgitation, but it is natural for the dog.

Some dogs can be reluctant to re-eat regurgitated food. They might feel they have done something wrong, and be a bit ashamed. You could try leaving your dog alone for a bit (with the regurgitation) and see if he eats it then. If not, let the stomach calm down for a bit and then offer some fresh food – he'll still be hungry.

I occasionally witness regurgitation when offering raw food, but only very infrequently. It is not something all dogs experience when starting a raw diet, and is not something to be overly concerned about unless it becomes persistent. It shouldn't be happening a lot, so do consult a vet if it becomes frequent. It may indicate an underlying problem.

Digested food which is brought up is vomit – a very different thing to regurgitation and veterinary consultation should be sought to help identify the cause. Sensible raw feeding should not result in vomiting; there is likely some sort of illness that is responsible.

WATER

You may notice that your dog isn't drinking quite as much water as he did when on a commercial diet. Don't worry – the raw diet has more water content than dry kibble, so he simply doesn't need to drink so much.

Obviously, he still should be drinking some water! Any symptoms of dehydration (loss of elasticity in the skin, sunken eyes, dry gums, thick saliva, collapsing) are signs of an underlying illness and need immediate veterinary consultation.

POO

You'll likely notice your dog's poo is smaller in size and less smelly than when on his commercial diet. This is because there are fewer fillers which go through the system undigested and which bulked out the poo. The high calcium content of an early raw-food diet can also make poo quite pale in colour, and means it will crumble into dust if you leave it on your lawn.

When you start hitting the 80%-10%-10% ratio, poo won't be quite so hard/crumbly/pale as at the start of the diet.

You might notice mucus in your dog's stools. This can be for various reasons. When just starting the diet, mucus forms due to toxins from the old diet being excreted. Mucus can also be a sign of inflammation of the digestive system, so if it appears after giving the dog a new food just cut back on this food for a bit until he gets more used to it. Persistent mucus and/or mucus which is accompanied by other signs of illness needs a vet consult.

RAW GUMS

Dogs who have been fed a commercial diet for some time are likely to have poor gum health, so when they start chomping on raw meat or bone you may see some raw or bleeding gums. It's like when people with not very good gums buy a new toothbrush – their gums bleed a little under the hardness.

A good raw diet will soon step up your dog's dental and gum health, and this bleeding will become a thing of the past. Keep an eye out, though, as persistent bleeding indicates an underlying issue which your vet will want to know about.

BONE FRAGMENTS

This can be a bit unsettling for a first-time raw feeder, but don't panic if you see bone fragments in your dog's poo or regurgitations.

Remember that your dog's stomach needs a bit of time to build up the enzymes required to fully digest bones; in the meantime, fragments may be expelled.

Chicken bones are soft, so fragments should not do any damage to your dog. But harder bones such as beef bones can do damage in fragment form; that's why it is a good idea to stick to chicken in the early stages.

You might see a bit of blood in your dog's poo with the bone fragments, though this is unlikely if you have only been feeding raw chicken bone. Bright red blood indicates a bit of tearing to the dog's lower intestine/rectum area. Provided it is only a little bit, this is nothing to panic about. Avoid bone in your next meal, add a bit of pumpkin and/or probiotic. You could also feed some bread before giving the next bone meal, as this helps to 'pad out' the bone and make it travel more smoothly through the system. Bread should not be a regular part of your dog's diet, though.

You are unlikely to see light red blood, but once your dog has hardened to the diet you shouldn't see any. If you do, it may be a sign that he has gotten hold of something he shouldn't have. Persistent appearance of red blood in the stool indicates an underlying digestive issue which you need to speak to a vet about.

Much darker, almost black, blood in the stool means that a more internal problem has occurred in your dog's digestive system. A sensible raw-food diet should never result in this, and I have certainly never seen it. But you should get your dog to a vet if you do observe dark blood in his stool.

11-   HOW MUCH TO FEED

The quantity of raw food you give will depend on your individual dog – athletic breeds will need more than couch-potato breeds, for example.

Here is a rough breakdown of the sort of quantity you might aim for at first.

For adult dogs over 10kg in weight:

Quantity is given as a percentage of your dog's ideal adult bodyweight. For example, a Newfoundland's adult bodyweight would be about 70kg, so 2% amounts to 1.4kgs of food each day (this breed comes under the 'less active' category).

Normal adult diet for average activity level – 2.5%-3% each day.

Adult diet for less active dogs – 2% each day.

Dogs which are on a weight-loss diet – 1.5% each day.

Very active dogs, or dogs which need to gain weight – 3 - 3.5% each day.

For adult dogs 10kg or less in weight:

9-10kgs – feed 3% of body weight each day.
5-8kgs – feed 5% of body weight each day.
3-4kgs – feed 7% of body weight each day.
1-2kgs – feed 10% of body weight each day.

For puppies, see the chapter 'FEEDING PUPPIES'.

As with any diet, you should monitor your dog's weight to make sure he is getting the right amount. You should be able to feel his ribs behind a covering of flesh, but ribs should not be visible (for most breeds). Your vet can help advise you on your dog's correct weight and any necessary dietary adjustments.

12-   FEEDING BONES

IS IT SAFE TO FEED BONES?

Yes, as long as they are raw. Never feed cooked bones. Be careful when purchasing bones – the prewrapped sorts you find in pet shops are cooked, which isn't necessarily obvious until you read the small print on the packaging. These are sold as recreational bones – to chew rather than to eat – but even as chewing toys, they are very hard and damaging to your dog's teeth. Smaller cooked bones are hard, brittle, and splinters can damage your dog's insides. A raw diet should consist only of raw meaty bones.

So long as you are selecting the right size and type of bone for your dog, raw bones are safe – and natural – to feed. Nevertheless, you will want to closely supervise your dog when he is eating bones. Make sure he isn't attempting to gulp down big bits of bone without crunching them down first. If he is, you should offer a larger variety of raw meaty bone.

Don't cut bones; buy bones which are appropriate in size for your dog without needing to be sawn into smaller pieces. Sawn edges can cause damage.

WHY FEED RAW BONES?

A big reason is because dogs love them. Eating a bone is good physical activity and releases endorphins.

Whole bones are also excellent for dental health. One of the most striking and immediate changes you will note in your dog when starting a raw food diet is that his teeth will look much cleaner than when he was eating commercial dry or wet food. This is thanks to the bones giving the teeth a good scrub. It also gives the jaw a workout, and helps keep gums healthy.

Bones also provide nutrition in the form of calcium, phosphorous, omega 3 fats, and glucosamine – as well as other species-appropriate forms of minerals and vitamins. Benefits include skin and joint health, and firmer stools.

WHAT BONES TO FEED

The best bones to feed are known as 'raw meaty bones'. This means bones which still have meat around them, not bones which have been scrubbed clean.

Chicken

Chicken bones are soft, and provide a good calcium source. When starting a raw diet, you should always begin with chicken bones only, because they are soft and allow your dog's enzymes to build up ready for harder bones.

Due to their softness, chicken bones are no good for teeth cleaning. They are not hard enough to scrub away the plaque and tarter on a dog's teeth, so you will eventually need to include harder bones in your dog's diet (see below).

Old dogs with fragile teeth may have to just stick to chicken bones – anything harder could damage their age-impaired teeth.

Chicken wings are good for smaller dogs, as are chicken necks.

Larger dogs will enjoy leg bones, breast quarters, and chicken carcasses.

Lamb

Once your dog has gotten used to his chicken bones, lamb is a good next step. Lamb bones are harder than chicken, but not so hard as beef. They are hard enough to improve dental health, unlike chicken bones.

Lamb ribs and necks are good to feed. Lamb necks tend to have a good bit of meat with them. Bigger, stronger dogs will do well with lamb leg bones.

Beef

Beef bones are harder than lamb bones, and give teeth a really good clean. However, due to their hardness I don't like to feed them too regularly. I only feed them every couple of weeks in order to prevent damage to my dogs' teeth. I feed lamb and chicken bones more frequently.

Do keep checking your dog's teeth, especially when feeding beef bones. If you notice any signs of teeth being worn down, revert to the softer chicken and lamb bones.

Beef ribs are best to eat. Marrow bones are fine for recreational use – dogs love them – but too hard to chew on and eat. Any weight-bearing bones in big animals like bovines are too hard for chewing and eating, so best to stick with ribs here.

Oxtail is good for reasonably strong chewers, but don't get oxtail which has been sliced up into little chunks.

Turkey

Turkey necks are good for medium to large dogs, as they are bigger than chicken necks. They are really meaty and not too hard.

I don't like feeding other turkey bones, such as legs, because turkeys tend to have very hard and sharp ligament tissue.

Duck

Duck bones are good for smaller dogs, though tend to be harder to get hold of than chicken and there's no particular reason to prefer them to chicken. These are softer bones and won't do much to help clean teeth.

WHAT SIZE BONES SHOULD I FEED?

You want bones which are too big to be gulped down without crunching up first, but not too hard for smaller or less-strong dogs.

So, you wouldn't give chicken wings to a Great Dane, but you also wouldn't give big beef ribs to a Jack Russell.

One rule-of-thumb I once heard was to only feed bones which are as big as your dog's head. I'm not sure this is particularly helpful; after all, none of the bones I feed are similarly shaped to my dog's head so it's hard to compare size! But it reinforces the point that you shouldn't feed bones which could be easily gulped down.

A basic breakdown might look like this:

Small dogs (up to 15kg): chicken wings and necks; lamb ribs and necks.

Medium dogs (15-35kgs): chicken legs, breasts, and carcasses; lamb ribs and necks, turkey necks, oxtail and maybe the occasional beef rib bone depending on your dog's strength – and the strength of his teeth.

Large dogs (35kgs +): chicken legs, breasts, and carcasses – or a whole chicken; turkey necks; lamb ribs and legs, oxtail and sometimes a beef rib bone.

You can give smaller dogs bigger bones like beef rib bones; they'll love gnawing the meat off them – but remove it before they can get too carried away with chewing the actual bone.

HOW MUCH BONE TO FEED?

Remember the golden ratio: 80% meat, 10% bone and 10% offal. You need to balance your feeding of raw meaty bones so that you're hitting the 10% bone proportion of the whole raw diet. The 10% is for the actual bone content, and doesn't include meat around the bone. I feed raw bones every two or three days.

Poo checking can help determine how close you are too hitting the balance. Poo which is consistently hard and crumbly can indicate too much bone being fed; conversely, soft runny poo probably means not enough. However, remember we feed lots of bone-in chicken meat at the start of the raw diet so don't worry if poo is hard at first. Furthermore, poo will often be hard and crumbly the day after you have fed bone. If it is consistently very hard, and causing constipation, you should lower the overall bone content of the diet.

WHERE TO BUY RAW MEATY BONES

Specialist raw-food merchants (see 'WHERE TO GET RAW FOOD') can supply you with a variety of raw meaty bones, but butchers and supermarkets are also good sources and they don't tend to be expensive. Some butchers are quite happy to hand out free bones, especially if you're a regular customer!
Just make sure you are buying raw, not cooked, bones. The packaged bones in pet shops are cooked – avoid.

STORING RAW BONES

It is fine to store raw meaty bones in the freezer, though you can feed them fresh.

They are best defrosted slowly overnight or in a freezer, and should be given to your dog within 24 hours of defrosting.

KNUCKLE BONES

These seem to be very commonly sold, and often seem to be offered by butchers when you ask about bones for dogs. But, these are weight bearing bones and not good for eating. Best to stick with the types suggested above.

CHECK YOUR DOG'S TEETH FIRST

A good tip before you first begin feeding raw meaty bones is to make sure your dog's teeth are already in good condition. Any teeth which are damaged won't get any better when they start crunching on bones. Get your vet to check if you can't do it yourself.

13-   FEEDING MEAT

We've covered raw bones, which make up 10% of the complete raw diet; now let's take a look at the meat which should constitute 80% of the diet.

Remember, some of the meat on your raw meaty bones will help make up the 80%; bear that in mind while balancing.

One thing to consider when you're shopping for your dog is that meat which appeals most greatly to humans won't necessarily be so thrilling for your dog. For example, a nice portion of chicken breast fillet might sound lovely to us, but it might be a bit bland and boring for your dog. Dogs like meats with different smells and textures – often ones which seem quite unpleasant to us.

Make sure you are only buying natural meat – no processed meat such as sausages, burgers, meatballs, etc.

With each ingredient I explain what vitamins and minerals are contained; see the chapter 'VITAMINS AND MINERALS: THEIR BENEFITS' for more detail on why these are valuable for your dog.

CHICKEN

Chicken meat is a good source of vitamins B3, B5, B6 and B12, protein, selenium, choline and phosphorous.

It has less saturated fat and cholesterol than red meats, which makes it good for weight control and for a healthy heart.

You can get chicken meat from your butchers or the supermarket, but your dog might also enjoy the minced chicken available from raw-food merchants. This is much cheaper to buy, and often contains 'other bits' of the chicken which make it more appealing (and nutritious) for your dog.

Chicken gizzards are also a good meat to feed. Although these are technically organs, they are quite meaty so can help make up the 80%. Gizzards are organs in the digestive tract of poultry which, similar to the stomach, help to grind up food. Your dog will likely find their texture and taste interesting, and they provide minerals such as zinc and iron. Some raw-food merchants supply these, or you can ask your butcher.

Salmonella does not pose the same risk to dogs as it does to humans. Dog's digestive systems are better designed to cope with bacteria than ours – for example, their saliva has strong anti-bacterial components, and their short digestive tracts don't give bacteria enough time to cause trouble.

Thought from Frank:

Chicken carcass is a personal favourite of mine. It's tasty, interesting to eat, and I can carry it off to a quiet corner of the garden to enjoy in peace. Tearing into a whole chicken carcass makes me feel as if I'm a proper wolf. Arooooooo...

BEEF

The nutritional quality of beef varies depending on how the cow it comes from was raised. Beef from pasture-fed cows is good, but is often difficult/expensive to source. Nevertheless, any chunks of beef you can get hold of will be better than the meat in commercial food.

Grass-fed beef provides vitamins B12, B3 and B6, protein, selenium, more iron than chicken, and zinc.

Raw-food merchants can normally provide nice big chunks of beef which your dog will likely enjoy tearing into more than minced beef. I sometimes get brisket cuts from the butchers for a treat, and supermarkets often have reductions on roasting joints.

LAMB

Quite a rich red meat, lamb is delicious for dogs but might be best to leave until he has gotten used to chicken and beef.

Lamb fat is one of the harder meat fats for a dog to digest; you might want to opt for leaner cuts wherever possible.

Lamb has lots of protein, and is a good source of vitamins B3 and B12, selenium, zinc and phosphorous.

TURKEY

A good mix – turkey is 70% white meat and 30% dark meat. It is a good source of protein, zinc, iron, potassium and phosphorous along with vitamins B3 and B6.

One benefit of turkey over chicken is that farming methods tend to be a bit more pleasant – turkey are often raised in a free-range environment, which can make for better meat.

PORK

Some raw feeders have concerns about feeding raw pork due to the parasite called Trichinella Spiralis which used to be prevalent in this meat. However, due to changing farming methods this parasite is no longer a big risk. I have fed raw pork with no problems. If you want to verge on the safe side, freeze your pork for one or two weeks before feeding it to kill off parasites.

However, pork is a fatty meat and some dogs do not digest it well. Try to find lean cuts or trim fat manually. Unfortunately, the same modern and intensive farming methods that have reduced the risk of parasites have also compromised the nutritional value of the meat.

Pork provides vitamins B1, B2, B6 and B12, iron, magnesium, zinc, potassium and protein.

GOAT

Worth picking up if you can find it – which might be tricky, but try asking your butcher, find an ethnic meat merchant, or order online. Goat is a very lean meat – less fat content and cholesterol than other meats, but higher in iron than beef. A good option for old dogs or dogs prone to weight gain.

It is a good source of vitamins B2, B3 and B12, protein, iron, zinc, phosphorous, copper and selenium.

FISH

Fish is a great whole-prey food – you can chuck a whole fish to your dog and he'll get the benefits of every bit of it, bones included. It is preferable to feed whole fish rather than filleted meat.

Fish is a very good ingredient of a raw diet because it is such a good source of omega-3 fatty acids which help keep skin and coat healthy, and support the immune system.

Always freeze raw fish for one to two weeks before feeding. Some raw fish, depending on where it is sourced, can contain parasites, but freezing kills them off and makes it perfectly safe for your dog.

Starting off with a whole fish might be a bit confusing for your dog, so perhaps try cutting it up into smaller bits so he can get the taste for it – but not so small that he gulps it down without chewing.

Most whole fish you'll find in the supermarket/fishmongers is fine for dogs – just avoid any types of fish that have hard spines on their backs. Salmon, trout, tuna, sardines and mackerel are good options to start with.

Don't overdo the fish – it contains an enzyme that breaks down vitamins, which can lead to vitamin deficiencies if a lot is fed.

RABBIT

Easily obtained from butchers – often as a whole prey – or gamekeepers, if you know any. Rabbit is a very powerful source of protein and iron. It also packs a lot of vitamins B12, B3, and selenium.

VENISON

A rich red meat very high in protein and low in fat. Unfortunately, it is quite difficult and expensive to obtain, unless you know any helpful gamekeepers.

HEART

Because they are muscles, beef and lamb hearts are similar to muscle meat but contain a lot of protein and particular nutrients such as coenzyme Q10; this supports cell and heart function. Heart meat also contains more collagen than other meats, which makes it good for joint support and skin condition.

You can often find beef and lamb hearts in larger supermarkets. Butchers will also sell them, as do raw-food merchants.

TRIPE

Tripe is a great food for dogs, but make sure you are feeding natural green tripe and not bleached tripe. This can make it a little harder to find – most butchers and supermarkets only sell bleached tripe. Raw-food merchants should be able to provide green tripe.

Tripe is the stomach lining of sheep and cattle. It is full of digestive enzymes which helped the animal it came from break down food, and will bring the same probiotic benefit to your dog. These enzymes have other wonderful powers, such as cleansing the blood.

Cooking destroys these fabulous enzymes, so make sure your tripe is raw as well as green.

It also absolutely stinks – but this makes it all the more exciting for your dog. I get my tripe from my raw-food merchant who, thankfully, cuts it up into chunks. Some dogs might enjoy tearing into tripe which hasn't been cut up, but only the stronger chewers – it's very tough.

Green tripe has a reputation for being a 'superfood' among raw feeders, and is well worth making the effort to obtain.

TONGUE

Tongue is fatty but is also another good source of protein, iron and zinc. Dogs seem to really enjoy it and it makes a good occasional ingredient. Supermarkets sell tongue meat, but it tends to be processed so try your butcher or order online.

LUNG

When I first started feeding raw meat and was cruising around my local butchers, one of them gave me a complementary bag of lung. It was quite a memorable experience, taking that lung out of its plastic bag at home and slicing it up – lung has a very odd consistency. Unfortunately, it hasn't proven popular whenever I have offered it.

Lung meat isn't particularly rich in vitamins, but it is a potent source of protein whilst being very lean indeed – so the ideal ingredient for dogs on a weight-loss diet.

FEET

Chicken, duck and turkey feet make for good occasional ingredients that dogs enjoy. They are a good source of glucosamine and chondroitin, which are good for maintaining healthy joints.

Pigs' trotters are also an enjoyable food for dogs with more bone content than duck/chicken feet and reliably available from Morrisons.

You might come across cow hooves, sometimes stuffed, sold by raw-food merchants – I avoid these, as I think these hooves are too hard and difficult to digest.

TRACHEA

A food which will interest your dog – trachea often comes with tantalising bits of meat attached, and the windpipe itself is nice and satisfying to chew on without being so strenuous as a bone.

Like lung, trachea provides a lot of protein with little fat. It is also a good source of glucosamine and chondroitin.
It can be quite difficult to obtain, though most raw-food merchants can supply it.

HOW TO BALANCE ALL THIS?

So you've got your freezer full of chicken, beef, tripe, heart, trachea etc. which can all contribute to the 80% of the overall raw diet. How do we know how much of each ingredient to feed? The simplest way is to imagine ingredients in terms of the proportion it makes of the animal it came from, and feed to your dog in similar proportion.

For example, the heart, proportionally, is a small part of the animal when compared to all the muscle meat. So you'd only feed a little bit of heart compared to muscle meat. Same with tripe, trachea, etc.

Let's say that the heart makes up 3% of the entire animal – heart should also be 3% of your raw food diet (more or less; this doesn't have to be pedantically precise!).
You do not have to try and feed all these ingredients every week – a good variety, fed over weeks or months, will be fine.
But good variety is key for an effective diet, so source as wide a range as possible.

Thought from Frank:

Personally, I don't enjoy the sensation of eating minced meat from a bowl. I don't know if it's the unpleasantness of having to shove my nose into the meat, or something about the shape of my mouth that just doesn't make eating from a bowl comfortable, but I prefer not to do it. Therefore, when I am served minced meat, I will often request that it be fed to me by a wooden spoon. My owner seems happy to oblige (though I don't know why he has to make those 'here come the choo-choo train' noises...). My friends might laugh at me, but they have to understand that each dog has his particular quirks; it's part of our charm!

14-   FEEDING OFFAL

For the final 10% of our raw-food diet, we need offal – which is a term for secreting organs.

Offal is a rich source of nutrients – so rich, that we should keep it to 10% of the overall diet so as not to overwhelm our dog's digestive systems.

The best place to get offal is your butcher or supermarket. This is because offal can harbour parasites, so we should purchase human-grade offal which has been inspected in a way that ensures it is free from such parasites.

LIVER

Half of the offal diet – so 5% of the overall diet – should be liver. It is healthy source of protein, fat and vitamin A as well as copper, iron, zinc, phosphorous, vitamin B3 and B12, and omega 3 and 6 fatty acids.

Do keep to the 5% - too much can lead to a vitamin-A overdose, resulting in various unpleasant health problems.
You are best to stick with lamb, beef, pork or chicken liver from your supermarket or butchers. It is not very expensive. Liver from game can have odd hard bits that make it dangerous to eat.

Most dogs will enjoy eating raw liver, though some seem to find its raw consistency unappealing. If your dog turns its nose up at your liver offering, try very lightly heating it in a hob or under a grill. Only heat it lightly or it will lose much of its nutritional benefit.

KIDNEY

Kidney provides very similar nutrition to liver, but has a different taste and consistency which may interest your dog.

SPLEEN

A great source of iron and vitamin C, but can be hard to find. You might have luck at a butchers, or at oriental food shops/markets. Spleen can also be ordered online.

BRAIN

Brain is a good source of B vitamins, selenium and copper as well as omega-3 fatty acids.

In Britain, only lamb and calf brains from animals under a year old have been classified as safe for human consumption. They are rather hard to get hold of. Your butcher is worth a shot and will at least them something to chuckle about when you ask. Specialist butchers, ethnic butchers and meat markets are the most likely source if you have access to any.

Remember to check that your brain comes from an animal under a year old, and don't purchase if there's any doubt.

PANCREAS

This contains similar nutritional benefits to other offal – rich in proteins, iron, omega-3 fatty acids and bringing benefit to immunity and digestion.

Pancreas is reasonably easy to get hold of, mainly from raw-food merchants. You can order it online.

TESTICLES

It's worth asking your butcher for testicles for amusement value alone, but if you don't have any luck there you will probably find these at ethnic butchers and certainly online from raw-food merchants.

They are a lean source of protein and zinc, and also contain potassium, sodium, magnesium, iron and phosphorous.

Thought from Frank:

Personally, I prefer my offal to be very lightly heated before I eat it. I make sure my owner doesn't do more than very lightly heat it, because I don't want any nutrients to be lost – or to get my mouth burnt.

15- FEEDING VEGETABLES AND FRUIT

BARF practitioners will mix fruit and vegetables into their dogs' meals in order to bring additional nutritional benefit – and this is the practice I have always followed.

I normally feed big dogs – 60-70kgs – and for them I add about 1 – 2 tablespoons of pureed fruit and/or vegetables into one of their daily meals (500g of meat).

For small dogs I feed a one or two heaped teaspoons; medium dogs one or two dessert spoons.

These are fairly conservative measurements; you could choose to feed more if you want to make the nutrients offered by fruit and vegetables a larger proportion of your dog's diet. I would not, however, make fruit and veg more than about 10% of the daily diet. Remember that in the wild, they would only be getting vegetable matter from the stomachs of their prey, so not vast quantities.

Do not feed a lot of any one particular type of fruit or veg. Feeding too much of a single ingredient can have harmful effects.

Introduce new ingredients in small amounts and watch for adverse reactions before upping the quantity.

Obviously, you don't have to try and get all these fruits and vegetables into every meal. I generally pick two or three types of fruit or veg, blend them up, and add them to my dogs' meals for the next couple of days (keeping the blended mix in a fridge). Then I repeat with a different mixture of fruits and veg, aiming for a good variety over the long term.

Don't try adding whole/sliced/chunked fruit and veg to your dog's meal – his digestive system cannot cope with it. Fruit and veg needs to be broken down in some way for him to cope with it. You can steam it, or lightly boil it, but I normally just give it a good long time in a food processor. The pureed fruit and veg is then broken down enough for my dogs' digestive systems to deal with.

However, many vegetables are actually more easily absorbed if they are steamed – in fact, steaming can release nutrients. So if you are prepared to go to the trouble of steaming, it may be the way to bring the maximum nutritional benefit to your dog.

Not all fruits and vegetables are safe for dogs to eat. See 'FRUITS AND VEGETABLES NOT TO FEED' for more on this.

Remember: don't feed too much of any single one of these – keep mixing up the variety.

VEGETABLES

Pumpkin

This comes first because it is a miracle worker when it comes to helping overcome digestive problems. Tinned pumpkin – pure, not pie mix – works absolute wonders whenever your dog has an upset stomach, thanks to its superb source of easily absorbed dietary fibre. Two even teaspoons for small dogs, two dessert spoons for medium dogs, and a heaped tablespoon for big dogs will do the trick.

Asparagus

Championed for its anti-inflammatory properties, asparagus is a terrific source of vitamin K, contains lots of vitamin B9 and copper, and is a decent source of many other nutrients such as vitamins B1, B2, B3 C, E and A, selenium, manganese, phosphorous, fibre, potassium, choline, zinc, iron and protein.

Beet root

Contains a good amount of vitamin B9 and manganese.

Broccoli

Be aware that a large amount of broccoli can cause a certain type of poisoning which leads to unpleasant gastric inflammation, but it is perfectly safe and healthy to feed broccoli in moderation. If you're really worried about gastric upsets, only feed the stalks – it's the florets which contain the irritant.

Broccoli packs a lot of nutrients, including: vitamins K, C, B1, B2, B5, B6, B9, some B3, and A; chromium, fibre, phosphorous, manganese, choline, potassium, copper, and some magnesium, protein, zinc, iron, calcium and selenium.

Brussels sprouts

Brussels sprouts are a very potent source of vitamins K and A. They also have a decent amount of manganese, fibre, choline, copper, potassium, phosphorous, iron, and vitamins B1, B6 and B9.

Cabbage

All types of cabbage have anti-oxidant properties and can be helpful for digestion. They are very good sources of vitamins K and C; they are also good for vitamin B6, manganese, fibre and potassium.

Carrots

Some dogs will appreciate a whole carrot for a treat – they can make quite nice chewing snacks, and might help give teeth a bit of a scrub. Freezing the carrot might make it a bit more tempting. One of Frank's favourite toys when he was a puppy was a frozen carrot tied to a piece of string. I would run around the garden holding the string; he did his best to chase the carrot – and then eat his 'prey'.

Not all dogs like chewing on a whole carrot, but they can still be blended into a meal.

Carrots have anti-oxidant properties, helping to protect against damage on the cellular level. They are also a very good source of vitamin A and lutein, which is good for eye health. Furthermore, carrots have quite a bit of vitamin B8, vitamin K, fibre, molybdenum, potassium and vitamin C.

Cauliflower

Cauliflower is a powerful source of vitamin C; it also contains some vitamin K, vitamins B5 and B6, potassium and fibre.

Celery

Can be soothing for the digestion, and is a good source of vitamin K and molybdenum.

Courgette/zucchini

Good for vitamins A and C, and potassium and fibre.

Cucumber

Very low in fat and oils, cucumber is another good, healthy ingredient. Recent studies have shown antioxidant and anti-inflammatory effects in animals. They have a lot of vitamin K and molybdenum along with some potassium, phosphorous, copper, manganese and magnesium, and some vitamins B1, B5, B8 and C.

Green beans

Green beans provide antioxidants and are a good source of vitamin K, manganese, fibre, vitamin C and vitamin B9.

Kale

Another good source of antioxidants, kale is also one of the most potent sources of lutein, which can support the health of the eye.

It's quite a tough leaf, so you might consider steaming it a bit to aid digestion; it should at least be blended thoroughly (same goes for all fruit and vegetables listed here).

Kale is a good source of vitamins K, A and C, and manganese and copper.

Lettuce

A good low-calorie food for dogs on a diet, lettuce is a potent source of vitamin A, vitamin K and vitamin B9. It also contains some fibre, vitamins B1, B2, B8 and C, manganese, potassium, copper and iron.

Some lettuce varieties are more nutritionally powerful than others; for example, romaine lettuce contains a great deal more vitamin C than your standard iceburg.

Okra

A great source of fibre, along with vitamins A, B9 and C, calcium and magnesium.

Peas

Shown to have anti-inflammatory and antioxidant benefits, peas are also a very good source of various nutrients. They have a lot of vitamins K, B1 and C, and a good amount of B6, B9, B2 and B3. They also have a lot of manganese, fibre, copper and phosphorous, and some protein, zinc, molybdenum, magnesium, iron, potassium and choline.

Spinach

A potent source of nutrients, which includes a type of lipid that is believed to protect the walls of digestive tracts – so spinach could be a good ingredient to use if your dog has any digestive problems.

Spinach is a good source of vitamins K, A, B2, B6, B9, E and C; it also has lots of manganese, magnesium, iron, copper, calcium and potassium.

Watercress

Believed to possess anti-inflammatory properties, watercress is a good source of vitamins B1, B2, B6, C, A and K, and manganese, phosphorous, potassium and calcium.

NIGHTSHADE VEGETABLES AND FRUITS

Vegetables and fruits which belong to the nightshade family have some inflammatory properties which can cause irritation to some dogs. When feeding these, start with small amounts and look closely for any adverse reactions such as sore spots around the mouth area or elsewhere on the skin, digestive trouble, and stiffness. Whilst most dogs don't encounter any problems, it is best to be careful and keep a sharp eye open. If your dog has underlying inflammatory-related conditions such as arthritis, you might want to avoid the fruits in this section.

Aubergine/eggplant

High in fibre, potassium, copper, manganese, and vitamins B1 and B6 as well as antioxidant properties, aubergine should be offered in very small doses at first – check for adverse reactions before increasing.

Bell pepper

Sometimes recommended for people suffering from arthritis due to their anti-inflammatory properties, bell peppers may also be a beneficial part of your dog's diet. Red, yellow or green bell peppers can be fed. Don't feed hot peppers.

They contain a lot of vitamin C and also provide vitamins A, E B6 and B9, molybdenum and fibre.

Start by feeding in very small amounts; check for adverse reactions before increasing quantity.

Tomato

Tomatoes are a good source of vitamins C, B8 and K as well as molybdenum, potassium, copper and manganese.

Beware – the plant material is toxic to dogs, including stem and leaves. The tomato fruit itself is fine.

POTATOES

A special mention for potatoes, because they can be fed to dogs along with the other vegetables and fruits listed above but have different preparation requirements.

Potatoes are also part of the nightshade family of plants so feed in small amounts at first, and watch for any adverse reactions. It's probably best not to feed them if your dog has kidney issues or any underlying inflammatory conditions such as arthritis. Sweet potatoes are not part of the nightshade family, so these concerns don't apply to them.

Whereas you don't have to cook the other vegetables listed, potatoes must be peeled and boiled in order to be safe for canine consumption. Whilst this point is argued – some say that only green potatoes are poisonous – the safest route is to boil and mash up your dogs' potatoes.

It is well worth the effort. Sweet potato is a wonderful aid to any dog suffering from digestive problems, and is almost as powerful as tinned pumpkin in this regard. It is a good alternative if you can't get hold of tinned pumpkin. A couple of heaped teaspoons of boiled and mashed sweet potato for smaller dogs, a couple of dessert spoons for medium dogs, and a couple of tablespoons for the big beasts will help firm up any loose stools.

Sweet potatoes are a potent source of vitamin A, unlike their white relatives. Both sweet and white potatoes are good for manganese, copper, vitamins B5 and B8, potassium, and fibre. They also have a lot of vitamin C, though this is lost through the cooking.

A SPECIAL MENTION FOR GARLIC

It is difficult to know whether to list this as a safe food or a potentially dangerous one. Research has condemned garlic as being poisonous to dogs; however, recent analysis into the studies that drew these conclusions have criticised their methods, claiming that excessive dosages and artificial means of feeding skewed the results against garlic's favour. Many raw feeders are keen proponents of garlic's tremendous health benefits and happily include it in their dogs' diets. You will likely want to do your own research before deciding for yourself.

Garlic has a lot of amino acids, sulphur, inulin, zinc, potassium and phosphorus. It has some vitamins A and C, calcium, magnesium, manganese, selenium, germanium and various B vitamins.

It can help circulation, has antioxidant and anti-inflammatory properties, aids digestion and helps purify blood, among other things.

FRUITS

Remember to bear in mind how dogs and their relatives would receive fruit in the wild — through the stomachs of their prey — and feed in corresponding quantities. Fruit should be pureed similarly to vegetables.

Apple

Good for vitamin C, fibre, calcium and phosphorous. The pips, however, contain cyanide — so remove the core and pips before blending.

Banana

Good for potassium, fibre and copper. High in sugar, so don't feed too frequently, and don't feed the skins – only the internal flesh.

Blueberries

This fruit, renowned for its antioxidant properties, will bestow health benefits on dogs as well as humans. Apart from being a good source of vitamin C and fibre, it will help support immune systems, and can also slow brain decay. Blueberries' antioxidants help to counter the effects of free radicals – these are a natural metabolic by product which cause damage on the cellular and molecular level.

Grapefruit

Good for vitamins C and B9, fibre, potassium and pectin. Has cancer-preventative properties and supports the immune system.

Mango

Provided the stone is removed, mangoes can be included in your dog's diet. They have a lot of fibre and vitamins A and C, along with some potassium, protein, magnesium, and vitamins K and B6.

Oranges

Good for vitamin C, folic acid, potassium and vitamin B1. Best not to feed the peel, as it can be hard work for the digestive system. Has cancer-preventative properties and supports the immune system.

Pear

Good for vitamin C, fibre, pectin and potassium.

Pineapple

A potent fruit which should be introduced carefully and only ever fed at moderate levels (though the same goes for all fruit and veg – we want to maintain a wide variety and never give too much of one particular ingredient). Pineapple has a lot of natural sugar and fibre, which can cause trouble with some dogs' digestive systems, so monitor carefully when first feeding it. It is a rich source of nutrients, containing vitamins C, B2, B3, B5, B6, B9 and B1, manganese, copper and bromelain. Only feed the flesh – don't include any of the husk when blending.

Raspberries

A nice light fruit with very high water content – good for weight-management diets. Raspberries have anti-oxidant properties and are packed with vitamin C, manganese and fibre. They have some copper and vitamin K, too.

Peaches
Stones must be removed before feeding – they contain cyanide. Otherwise, a very healthy fruit whose benefits your dog can enjoy too; peaches contain carotenoids which may help with fighting infections. They have a lot of vitamin C and A, and high levels of fibre.

Strawberries

Good for vitamin C, fibre, vitamin B9, potassium and magnesium. A good source of antioxidants.

16- OTHER INGREDIENTS AND SUPPLEMENTS

OILS

It's a very good idea to supplement your dog's diet with a good oil, as they offer concentrated sources of valuable nutrients.

Salmon oil

A very popular supplement due to its prominent health benefits. Salmon oil is a great source of omega 3 and 6 fatty acids, which improve skin and coat condition, support the immune system, can support brain function and possess anti-inflammatory properties, among over things.

It's worth getting a good quality salmon oil. There are different methods of extracting the oil from the fish, and cheaper oils use methods which can compromise the integrity of those all-important fatty acids.

You can find salmon oil easily online; many pet shops and raw-food merchants also sell it, but check it is of good quality first.

Feed 1 teaspoon of salmon oil for small dogs, 2-3 teaspoons for medium dogs, and 4 teaspoons for big dogs, with one meal each day.

Coconut oil

Coconut oil is a very potent source of healthy saturated fats – the type of fat we want to include in our dogs' diets. It is lauded for its anti-viral, anti-bacterial and anti-fungal properties. Coconut oil can also be really good for skin and coat condition, and aids digestion.

Start by feeding very small amounts, then work up to a similar dosage to salmon oil (see above). You can give up to 1 teaspoon per 5kgs of dog weight, but reduce in the event of any adverse reactions, such as diarrhoea.

Coconut oil can be purchased from supermarkets, raw-food merchants (it's a popular supplement) or online.

Flaxseed oil

If your dog doesn't like salmon oil, flaxseed is a good alternative as it brings very similar nutrients and benefits. Generally, dogs digest animal-based nutrients better than plant-based ones, so salmon oil is best to try first.

Flaxseed oil contains the same sort of fatty acids as salmon oil, but may have a preferable taste. Again, quality is important as flaxseed can become rancid if it isn't stored or packaged well. Purchase online, but research the brand and check reviews to make sure you are getting a good quality source.

Feed in similar doses to salmon oil (see above).

GRAINS

Now we enter a bit of a war zone. For many, the idea of feeding grains is absolute anathema to the whole concept of raw feeding – we are trying to get away from the cereal-filled diets subjected to our dogs by commercial food.

Others will say that a good quality grain will give a healthy source of carbohydrates, to which you might argue that dogs don't actually need carbohydrates – they derive their energy from proteins and fats.

It's up to you to pick a side. Whether you choose to feed grains or not, you are not going to do any harm either way. Dogs do get enough energy from other sources, but a good quality carbohydrate can give a boost to their energy, too.

The main issue is with quantity. Carbohydrates have a bad reputation in the dog food world because they make up such a large proportion of cheap commercial foods in the form of poor quality grains (kernels, pods, husks, etc. which are hard to digest). Dog food companies love them because they are cheap and bulk up food nicely, but it is not good for a dog when grain carbohydrates take up the main portion of the diet.

Always remember the way dogs would ingest grains in the natural world – through the stomachs of their prey – and feed in corresponding amounts. I would not allow grains to become more than about 10% of the daily diet. The bulk of a dog's energy should be derived from meat sources, as this is what they are naturally designed to digest.

If you do feed grain as part of your dog's diet, stick to simple, easily digestible carbohydrates. Brown rice is good (it hasn't been subjected to the same degree of processing as white rice). Boil for twenty minutes and allow to cool. You can mix other ingredients into the rice – some nice probiotic yoghurt, or a mix of pureed fruit and vegetables. You can mix the rice with meat, too.

Rolled oats are also good. Leave them to soak in a bowl of water or unpasteurised milk (never give your dog pasteurised milk, or you will discover how explosively incapable they are of handling it) in the fridge overnight before serving. Add some yoghurt and a bit of natural honey, along with an oil supplement, for a nice breakfast.

Don't feed 'raw' grains – e.g., rice which hasn't been cooked or oats which haven't been soaked. The stomach will have to work too hard to digest it, and irritation will be the likely result.

OTHER

Egg

It's safe to feed a couple of raw, whole eggs each week. The nutritional quality of the egg depends on how well the chicken that laid it was fed, so it's best to source nice organic eggs from pasture-fed hens. Eggs provide protein, amino acids, choline, selenium, molybdenum, and vitamins B2, B8 and B12.

The shells provide calcium, and are a good alternative source for this mineral if you have a dog who struggles with bone. It is best to crush up the shells into a powder, as this makes it more easily absorbable for your dog's digestive system.

Raw eggs are safe in moderate amounts. They do contain an enzyme blocker which can cause trouble in large amounts. Cooking the egg prevents this, so you can do that if you are concerned. One egg a week for small dogs, and two for medium to large dogs should be absolutely safe, though. You can feed both the white and the yolk – just mix it into one of your dog's meals along with the powdered shell.

If you're using eggs from a shop, be aware that these are often sprayed with certain chemicals to treat the shells and make them look nice and shiny – rinsing the shell may or may not remove these chemicals. Organic eggs are the best option.

Kelp

Kelp powder is a popular supplement which can often be found in raw-food merchants, health-food shops, or online. Kelp is a good source of iodine, which helps support glandular health. Kelp also helps skin condition, and provides iron and calcium.

Half a teaspoon of powdered kelp a day will be fine for small dogs, and a whole teaspoon for larger dogs.

Turmeric

Turmeric has good anti-inflammatory properties and is considered to be just about the best natural remedy for dogs who suffer from stiff joints and inflammatory conditions such as arthritis. It can also soothe digestion.

Give ¼ teaspoon for each 5kgs of your dog's weight each day. Only use pure turmeric powder – health-food shops are a good place to get this or order online.

Glucosamine, chondroitin and methylsulfonylmethane.

If your dog suffers from orthopaedic conditions such as arthritis or hip/elbow dysplasia, you will want to supplement his diet with glucosamine, chondroitin and methylsulfonylmethane. These compounds serve as building blocks of joint tissue, and supplementing them can really help to ease the discomfort of dogs with orthopaedic illness. You might also want to offer these supplements if you have a dog of a breed prone to orthopaedic issues, such as large-breed dogs, as a preventative measure. For example, I give my Newfoundland these supplements on a daily basis not because he has any joint problems, but to help prevent any occurring.

Glucosamine and chondroitin can be sourced naturally – chicken and duck feet contain it as well as trachea. Methlysulfonylmethane is present in certain fruits and vegetables, such as tomato. However, I believe that in order for them to have any real beneficial effect, these supplements need to be offered in a concentrated manner. The downside of this is that it can get expensive, and it is hard to find a source which contains all three of these joint-supporting supplements. Riaflex is the best I have found, and it is available online – but brace yourself for the cost!

Ester-C

Ester-C is a more easily absorbable form of vitamin C. The necessity or benefit of supplementing a diet with Ester-C is somewhat debatable, as dogs conveniently produce their own vitamin C. So why give more?

I give large-breed dogs supplemented Ester-C because it is known to support joint health. Some research has even found that it can prevent orthopaedic issues such as hip/elbow dysplasia if introduced to the dog at an early enough stage (this has to be a very early, even pre-natal, stage!).

Vitamin C is also really helpful for dogs who are sick or stressed, so it might be a good thing to supplement if your dog is under the weather. Ester-C is the best form of vitamin C to give as a supplement, because it is so much more easily absorbed than straightforward vitamin C. This means the kidneys won't be overstrained, as they might be if you were giving increased amounts of straight vitamin C.

Ester-C can be obtained from health-food shops, or ordered online. It is hard to find the right sort of dosage for dogs. I only give it to big dogs (50kg+) to support their orthopaedic health, and they get two 500mg tablets each day (simply dropped into their meals).

If you want to supplement with Ester-C at its most potent healthy dosage, start by feeding a small amount and gradually increase the amount each day. When your dog starts to get runny poo, you have gone beyond the tolerated dose of Ester-C. Simply dial the dosage down a little, and keep offering that as the daily amount.

Probiotics

A good probiotic can help support gut flora and be very beneficial to the smooth running of your dog's digestive system.

Low-fat or fat-free Greek yoghurt can supply good probiotics; I prefer to use natural goats' yoghurt, though it's a little more expensive.

You can find either in supermarkets. One teaspoon for small dogs, a dessert spoon for medium dogs, and a tablespoon for large dogs added to a daily meal is all you need.

Herbs

Herbs contain antioxidants and can help soothe digestion. You can give dried herbs or fresh (in which case they should be blended in with your fruit/vegetable puree). A single pinch for small dogs, two pinches for medium dogs, and three for large dogs is a good dosage.

Oregano, basil, parsley, rosemary and peppermint are some of the herbs which are safe to give to dogs.

17- VITAMINS AND MINERALS: THEIR BENEFITS

Provided you are feeding a varied diet, you should have absolutely no worry about any nutritional deficiency and you don't need to keep a precise account of the quantities in which your dog is receiving all the different vitamins and minerals. This section might be helpful, however, if you want to tailor your dog's diet with focus on specific nutritional benefits. (See also 'TAILORING DIET'.)

Vitamin A

Important for proper metabolic function. Signs of vitamin-A deficiency include: poor coat and skin condition, weakened vision.

Potent sources: Liver, carrot, lettuce, sweet potato.

Vitamin B1

Important for converting carbohydrates to energy, vitamin B1 is needed for effective functioning of the heart, muscles and nervous system. Signs of vitamin-B1 deficiency include: general weakness, seizures, lack of coordination.

Potent sources: pork, fish, brussels sprouts, oranges, pineapple, rice.

Vitamin B2

Supports skin and coat condition, production of red blood cells, and metabolic function. Signs of vitamin-B2 deficiency include: dry skin, weakness, fatigue.

Potent sources: pork, fish, asparagus, broccoli, spinach, peas, watercress, pineapple, egg.

Vitamin B3

Supports digestive function, helps produce energy from food, and maintains skin condition. Signs of B3 deficiency include: diarrhoea, bad breath, excess drool.

Potent sources: meat, fish, spinach, pineapple.

Vitamin B5

Supports healthy metabolic function.

Potent sources: chicken, fish, broccoli, sweet potatoes, pineapple.

Vitamin B6

Supports good skin condition, immunity, and production of red blood cells. Signs of B6 deficiency include: weakness, seizures.

Potent sources: meat, fish, egg, peas, spinach, aubergine, rice.

Vitamin B8

Important for healthy metabolic function.

Potent sources: carrots, tomatoes, sweet potatoes, eggs.

Thought from Frank:
Honestly, who cares about all this vitamin mumbo-jumbo? So long as you keep feeding me a varied diet, I know I'll be getting all the vitamins and minerals I need.

Well, some people might be interested…

Vitamin B9

Important for digesting proteins, production of red cells, and for proper tissue growth.

Potent sources: liver, asparagus, beet root, strawberries, egg, pumpkin.

Vitamin B12

Important for proper blood production and for supporting the nervous system.

Potent sources: meat, fish, liver, eggs.

Vitamin C

Manufactured autonomously by the dog's liver, vitamin C contributes to collagen formation, making it important for healthy skin and joints and for an effective immune system. Supplementation of a good source of vitamin C, such as Ester-C, can be beneficial, particularly for dogs suffering from/prone to joint disorders.

Signs of deficiency include joint pain and poor immunity.

Potent sources: spleen, carrots, oranges, cauliflower, bell peppers.

Vitamin E

Serves as an antioxidant, preventing damage on the cellular and molecular level.

Potent sources: asparagus, bell peppers, spinach.

Bromelain

An enzyme with powerful anti-inflammatory properties, and helps with tissue healing.

Potent sources: pineapple.

Calcium

Maintains healthy bones and teeth. Excessive or insufficient calcium can lead to improper skeletal development in puppies.
Potent sources: bones, eggshell.

Choline

Good for brain and nerve function. Helps to prevent cognitive decay in older dogs. Potent sources: meat, liver, eggs.

Copper

Supports the formation of collagen as well as bone and joint tissue. Serves as an antioxidant, and supports the production of red blood cells.

Potent sources: liver, fish, brain, rice, peas, spinach, kale, aubergine, banana.

Fibre

Supports healthy digestive function, among other things. Constipation or loose stools can be due to an imbalance of fibre.

Potent sources: pumpkin in my experience is the greatest source of beneficial fibre. Any digestive problems that manifest in loose or excessively firm stools can be helped with pumpkin. Okra, aubergine, sweet potato and banana are among other good sources of fibre.

Iron

Important for effective blood function. Deficiency results in anaemia, the symptoms of which include weakness, improper growth, and susceptibility to stress and illness.

Potent sources: liver, meat, fish, dark green vegetables.

Magnesium

Necessary for the production of protein, metabolic function, and bone growth. Deficiencies are rare, but indicated by muscle trembling, weakness, and changes in behaviour such as the onset of depression.

Potent sources: pork, spinach, peas, fish.

Manganese

Important for proper protein and carbohydrate function, and for the production of energy. Deficiency is very rare but can result in growth and reproductive abnormalities.

Potent sources: green vegetables, eggs, grains.

Molybdenum

Helps digestion. Potent sources: cucumber.

Phosphorous

Important for energy storage and transfer, cell-membrane integrity and bone strength. Deficiency is very rare in dogs because phosphorous is so abundant in the canine diet, but would likely manifest in the form of skeletal malformation.

Potent sources: meat, offal, eggs.

Potassium

Important for nerve function, muscles and metabolic enzymes. Signs of deficiency include: heart problems, weakness, loss of appetite, stunted growth. Deficiency can be brought on by prolonged bouts of diarrhoea and vomiting.

Potent sources: potassium is widely available and deficiency shouldn't occur in a balanced diet, but banana, potato, peas, carrots and apple are among some good sources of it.

Selenium

An antioxidant which can have a lot of health benefits. It prevents cellular damage and can contribute to the prevention of cancer, heart disease and skin conditions.

Potent sources: meat, fish, egg, spinach.

Zinc

Performs various vital metabolic functions including but not limited to cellular reproduction, immunity and hormone production. Signs of deficiency include hair loss along with lesions and scaling on the skin in some dog breeds.

Potent sources: meat and bone.

18- FRUITS AND VEGETABLES NOT TO FEED

Until more research is done on dogs and their digestion, we won't know for sure the entirety of foods that are unsafe for them. In the meantime, it's best to play it safe. Some of the foods listed here are definitely unsafe for dogs; some might possibly be unsafe – only by avoiding these foods altogether can we be sure that we are risking our dogs' safety.

This list should be reasonably comprehensive but always research carefully before you feed a new fruit or vegetable to your dog.

Toxic or partly toxic to dogs:

Grapes

Raisins

Anything similar to grapes and raisins (prunes, dates, etc). Currants (both black and red).

Onion

Chives

Apricot, cherry, plum, nectarine, peach: need to be careful with these because the stones and plant material are toxic. The fruit flesh itself is safe.

Persimmons (toxic seeds).

Mushrooms

Green-skinned potatoes

Rhubarb (causes calcium deficiency in dogs)

Avocado (contains persin which can cause diarrhoea, heart congestion and other unpleasantness in dogs).

Nuts (some are safe for dogs, but many are not. Best to avoid altogether, as they bring little nutritional benefit for dogs).

19-   EXAMPLE MENUS

Let's take a look at what a full meal plan might look like for some different sizes of dogs. These example menus assume a dog has already been introduced to the raw diet – see 'HOW TO START'.

SMALL DOG (~7kgs, e.g. Jack Russell, small terrier.)

We're looking to feed about 5% of the overall adult weight for an adult dog (see 'HOW MUCH TO FEED'), so this amounts to about 350g per day for a dog of 7kgs in weight, or about 2.5kgs per week.

We need to feed 80% meat, 10% offal and 10% bone (percentages are of total amount fed, NOT percentage of body weight). Remember, we don't have to meet that ratio every day – try to strike that balance over a week or so. We'll look to feed about 250g of offal each week, which could form the bulk of one meal.

For bones, we'll take our pick from chicken wings or necks, and lamb ribs or necks. Remember, chicken bone is too soft to help dental health, so we'll want to offer some lamb occasionally.

Feed in one meal or split into two.

Day 1: 340g beef (chucks or mince), 2 teaspoons of pureed fruit and vegetable (let's say spinach and apple, pips removed), a splash of salmon oil.

Day 2: 4 chicken wings (each about 90g in weight with skin, about 20-30g of bone). If your dog is trying to gulp down the wings too quickly, give something bigger like a chicken quarter but remove when the dog has reached daily weight limit.

Day 3: 125g liver, 220g heart and green tripe with 2 teaspoons vegetable/fruit puree (different fruit and veg to the previous), salmon or other oil splashed on top.

Day 4: 340g turkey/pork/other meat, 2 teaspoons vegetable/fruit puree (again different types), splash of oil, and this time chuck an egg in there with eggshell powdered on top.

Day 5: lamb neck (with bone in). These tend to be big, so let your little dog tear away at it but remove when he has had his daily fill. This should give the weekly 10% requirement for bone, along with day 2's chicken wings, depending on how much of the neck your dog has eaten.

Day 6: 125g kidney (this gives us the remaining 5% offal requirement), 220g different type of meat (chicken gizzard or heart) with fruit/veg mixture and oil splashed on.

Day 7: give some green tripe, about 200g or so, along with some other meat and a couple of teaspoons of vegetable/fruit puree. Could give another chicken wing or neck if your dog didn't eat much of the neck bone on day 5.

Key points are to keep it varied, and to keep in mind the proportions. Remember a wild dog would get the fruit/vegetable content of its prey's stomach, which isn't much of the overall prey, so we feed fruit and veg in corresponding proportions (a teaspoon or two per day).

You can balance it differently – e.g. one meal of just offal, but no more offal for the rest of the week. Just observe how well your dog handles this by looking at his poo – if it's really dark and runny, it's best to split the offal across the week next time.

Strive for balance over the course of weeks – for example, if we follow the above for one week, we'll give fish and other types of meat in the next week.

Take care when balancing bone content. The 10% is for bone material only, it's not 10% raw meaty bones – because then the meat will be eating into the 10%. For example, for the dog above we need to feed about 120g of bone a week to hit 10% bone content in a week. But if we feed 120g of chicken wings, we're falling short of the 10% because there is meat and skin as well as bone on the wing. If in doubt, it's best to feed a bit too much bone than too little, as dogs can excrete natural calcium. If poo is really hard and causing constipation, just back off the bone for a bit.

Add other supplements (see relevant chapter) at your discretion. For example, you might chuck in a pinch of kelp here and there.

MEDIUM DOG (~30kgs, e.g. collie, retriever, setter)

We're again looking to feed 2.5-3% of adult body weight for a full-grown adult dog, so in this case we'll be wanting to feed 750-900g per day, or about 5.2-6.3kgs each week.

That means about half a kilo of bone and half a kilo of offal across the week.

Again, this can be fed in one meal or split into two or three. Some dogs don't do well if given too much food at once. A meal at breakfast and a meal in the evening works well, as does an early evening meal followed by a later supper.

Day 1: 1 chicken carcass, 400-500g meat (any variety) minced or chunks with 3-4 teaspoons of vegetable/fruit puree, a splash of oil (coconut, salmon, or flaxseed).

Day 2: 300g green tripe, 300g heart, beef trachea, maybe a couple of gizzards.

Day 3: another 400-500g meat and fruit/veg mix with oil, a different protein source this time. Chuck an egg into it. 200-300g liver and maybe a few duck feet.

Day 4: some whole fish, a lamb neck, some more heart or tripe. Should be 750-900g overall.

Day 5: 400-500g meat and fruit/veg mix with oil, again a different variety. Could throw a bit of yoghurt into it (goats' yoghurt or low-fat/fat-free Greek yoghurt). 300g kidney.

Day 6: Whole prey rabbit if you can get it, or another 400-500g meat/veg/oil mix. More tripe, heart or fish to make up the 750-900g.

Day 7: 400-500g meat/veg/oil mix, with an egg. A turkey neck or two, or chicken breast quarter.

Again, add your chosen supplements at your discretion. For some dogs, this sort of menu might be a bit rich, in which case I'd look to replace some of the meat with a bit of good-quality grain once or twice a week (grain should not be more than 10% of the weekly diet, though).

BIG DOG (~60kg, e.g. Newfoundland, mastiff, wolfhound)

2.5-3% guides us to 1.5-1.8kg a day, or about 10-12kg per week. Bone and offal should therefore make up about a kilo each per week.

Every day you could give a mix of 500g meat (chicken/turkey/beef/lamb etc.) aiming to change the protein source throughout the week. Mix with this a tablespoon or two of vegetable and fruit, pureed, again varying the types of fruit and veg as much as possible. Twice a week add an egg, with shell, to this mix. Add a few splashes of oil to it each day, along with any of your other chosen supplements. Add some yoghurt a couple of times a week.

In addition to that meat mix:

Day 1: chicken carcass, 300-400g green tripe, 300-400g meat cuts (beef chunks, turkey steaks, etc.)

Day 2: 500g liver, 300g heart, beef trachea, whole fish.

Day 3: whole prey such as rabbit.

Day 4: 500g meat cuts, turkey neck, duck feet, gizzards.

Day 5: 500g kidney, 300g tripe, a whole fish or two.

Day 6: big lamb neck, 300g heart, 300g other meat cuts.

Day 7: lamb or beef rib, some lung, or tongue, the rest meat cuts.

Thought from Frank:

I have more fish than is recommended in this example. In fact, I enjoy a daily breakfast of fish with a little rice that has goats' yoghurt and tinned pumpkin mixed into it. All dogs are different; that's just my particular taste.

All dogs are indeed different, so see how your dog responds to the diet and adjust accordingly. Low-energy dogs might need the quantity reduced to manage their weight properly. Some dogs might struggle with the quantity of offal suggested above, so lower accordingly. The next chapter goes into more detail about how to monitor and adjust the diet.

20-   MONITORING DIET

By keeping a close eye on how your dog responds to the food he receives in his diet, you can make changes and adaptations where necessary. It is best to introduce new ingredients slowly and separately so you will have a good idea of what new ingredient might be responsible for any adverse reaction you observe.

WEIGHT

Your vet can help you judge whether your dog is at the correct weight for his age and breed, but a rough guidance is that you should be able to feel your dog's ribs beneath a layer of flesh when you hold his sides, but not be able to see his ribs when you look at him.

When you start raw-food diet, some weight change might occur as you get used to feeding the right quantity, so keep an eye on weight with your vet's help.

ITCHING

If you notice your dog has started to itch more than usual, this is a likely sign that he is suffering an allergic reaction to a new ingredient in his diet.

If you have been introducing new ingredients one at a time, then the culprit should be easy to identify, and you can remove it from the diet.

Otherwise, you will have to go back to basics. Fast your dog for a day, then feed simple meals of bone-in chicken. Add new ingredients slowly until the itching starts again; this should give you a clear idea of what is causing the itching and you can remove it from the diet.

GAS

Normally, you will notice a striking decrease in unpleasant aromas emitted by your dog when you switch from commercial to raw food. However, cruciferous vegetables (broccoli, cauliflower, brussels sprouts, cabbage) and nightshade plants (tomatoes, potatoes, aubergines, bell pepper) can lead to gassiness so you should cut down on these ingredients if things are getting a bit windy.

POO

Let's return to our favourite subject. We have already discussed some of the changes in your dog's poo which you can expect when starting a raw diet, but studying poo can also be a good way of monitoring how well the raw diet is working for your dog. Here are some things to look out for:

Consistency

A big determiner in the consistency of your dog's poo is the amount of calcium he is receiving in the diet. If you're consistently seeing soft stools, you might try upping the bone content. Conversely, if your dog is producing a lot of very hard stool, you may need to back off the bone quantity.

Very loose stools are often a sign of digestive upset. Fast for a day, then go back to simple meals of bone-in chicken supplemented with some tinned pumpkin. Persistent loose stool or diarrhoea needs a vet's consult.

Mucus

It's quite easy to spot mucus in poo – it has an oily, snotty appearance. This is something you'll likely see once in a while, and isn't too much of a concern unless it is very frequent or very abundant.

Mucus in the poo is a sign that the digestive system has been working hard and has become a bit inflamed. This could be due to a new ingredient which you have introduced, in which case you might want to reduce the quantity of that ingredient until your dog's system becomes more accustomed to it.

You can offer certain foods to help ease your dog's digestion if he is getting mucus in his poo – try tinned pumpkin, celery, cucumber or carrots. A good source of probiotics could also help.

Dark-brown, loose stool

This is often an indication that your dog is receiving too much offal in his diet, especially if you're seeing this sort of consistency frequently. Check your proportions – remember to keep offal to 10% of the overall diet.

Orange/yellow stool

Often comes if the dog has eaten a lot of chicken. If you see this a lot, it might be a good idea to widen the variety of meat sources you offer.

Final word about poo

I am probably guilty of becoming a bit obsessive over my dogs' poo. We should remember that when feeding a good varied raw diet, the sorts of poo we are going to see will vary too. After a bone day, poo is going to be harder; after feeding offal, we'll see darker poo. These sorts of variations are fine and nothing to be concerned about. If every day you are seeing a similar type of poo, then it might be a sign that more variety is needed in the diet.

Consult your vet with any concerns.

21-   TAILORING DIET

Because we have full control over the ingredients our dogs receive in their diets, we have exciting opportunities to tailor for specific needs. Let's look at some example scenarios and how we can adapt diet accordingly.

OLD DOGS

In old age, dogs can start to develop quite a complex range of health issues. Reduced enthusiasm for exercise can make them prone to weight gain. Orthopaedic wear can lead to arthritis. Eyesight deteriorates. Brain function can also deteriorate, and you might see the onset of dementia. Tailoring our raw diet can help prolong the onset or worsening of these conditions.

To counter weight gain, we shouldn't just leap to the conclusion that old dogs should be fed less food, or lower-calorie food. Recent research points to the fact that old dogs actually need a high protein intake to prevent illness. Raw, unprocessed foods are undoubtedly best due to their high moisture content which puts less strain on digestive and metabolic systems. Furthermore, this diet provides better quality protein than processed foods.

So, whilst we might start feeding a little less when our dog enters old age (see 'HOW MUCH TO FEED') we shouldn't drop it off too much.

Lean cuts of meat are ideal because they provide high protein with less fat. Poultry is good, goat is brilliant if you can find it. Any meat with some fat trimmed is fine.

To support joint condition and slow the onset of arthritis, you can increase the intake of food containing glucosamine and chondroitin, important building blocks of joint tissue. Feet and trachea are good sources; you might also look to add a supplement such as Riaflex (see 'OTHER INGREDIENTS AND SUPPLEMENTS').

Some ingredients, such as carrot and kale, have properties which are good for supporting eye health so you could make these a more regular part of the diet. Keep up the 10% offal ratio; the vitamin A in this will also promote eye health.

The nutrient choline is important for supporting brain function; so feeding good sources of choline could help slow the onset of dementia. Eggs, salmon oil and blueberries are among the ingredients which can support healthy brain function; try making these a regular part of an older dog's diet.

Make sure your older dog is getting a good amount of antioxidants as this will protect him from illnesses which his old age makes him increasingly susceptible toward, and may even protect from the onset of cancers. Blueberries, raspberries, strawberries, and sweet potato (always cooked) are among the ingredients rich in antioxidants.

BIG DOGS

Very large breeds of dog have quite specific nutritional needs during the stage of their skeletal development. This means that during their growth period, you need to watch calcium levels as closely as possible. The skeletal growth stage normally lasts until about 18 months of age, at which point the skeleton is fully formed, but check with your particular breed.

Too much calcium can lead to excessively rapid development of bone tissue; this can result in orthopaedic conditions such as hip and elbow dysplasia. On the other hand, not enough calcium is going to cause insufficient bone development.

Phosphorous also plays a role in proper skeletal development, though research is more contradictory here. Generally, a diet which contains too much or not enough calcium or phosphorous, or an imbalance between the two, can lead to malformed skeletal development in large-breed dogs.

Ideally you want a diet with about 1% to 1.4% overall calcium, and slightly less phosphorous. This is difficult to accurately judge with a raw food diet. How much calcium is in any particular bone? And how can we keep track of this alongside other sources of calcium in the diet such as vegetables, yoghurt, eggs, etc.?

If you can keep careful account of the bone content in the raw diet, keeping it to the 10% ratio, you should be okay. Raw meaty bones balance out calcium with phosphorous that comes elsewhere in the meat diet nicely, and the 10% should provide the right quantity of calcium for proper development.

Growing puppies can excrete excess calcium, so it is best to verge on the generous side if you are in doubt. However, synthetic calcium is very difficult for them to excrete, so make sure you are supplying natural calcium in the form of raw meaty bones rather than synthetic supplements.

There is always the option of using a high quality commercial food during your large-breed puppy's growth stage and then switching to raw once skeletal growth is complete. Very good-quality foods, such as Orijen, have well-balanced calcium levels and this might make you more comfortable than trying to balance it yourself. Just don't subject your dog to a poor-quality food, and be careful when purchasing. There are many foods which are marketed as being wonderfully healthy (some which are championed by vets) that are in fact full of unhealthy grains and poor meat sources.

A good way to tailor a raw diet for your large breed dog is to offer a regular, good source of glucosamine and chondroitin to support their orthopaedic health. Large-breed dogs are particularly prone to orthopaedic issues; glucosamine and chondroitin support healthy joint function. Duck feet are a nice source, as are trachea. Also very beneficial is a maintenance dosage of a supplement such as Riaflex, which offers a pure, concentrated source of glucosamine, chondroitin and methylsulfonylmethane.

ANXIOUS DOGS

Interesting research is illuminating the possible benefits dietary adjustment can have for dogs that suffer from anxiety and stress. Whilst a couple of new ingredients aren't going to cure these conditions, you might notice some benefit.

An article published in the *Journal of Veterinary Behaviour* reported on the calming effect of substances called L-tryptophan and alpha-casozepine, finding them to reduce anxiety and stress in dogs.

L-tryptophan has quite a wide bioavailability – free-range eggs, wild-caught fish, pasture-fed beef, peas, bananas and yoghurt are good sources, so try increasing the proportion of these in your anxious dog's diet.

Alpha-casozepine is a bit more exclusive, being derived from bovine milk. If you can find a source of unpasteurised cow's milk, great. But don't try giving your dog pasteurised milk (which is the only type you'll find in shops) as he will not tolerate it. Things get very explosive in the rear-end department if a dog gets hold of too much pasteurised milk.

Thought from Frank:
Yes, I do still remember that time you thought it would be okay to soak my porridge oats in milk from the supermarket – and so does the neighbours' front lawn...

ITCHY DOGS

Most dogs, once settled on a raw-food diet, become freed from itchiness and dull coat/dry skin conditions that can plague them when on commercial foods. However, if your dog still gets bothered by dry itchy skin and a dull coat, here are some good ingredients to boost his diet:

Pork, fish, asparagus, broccoli, spinach, peas, watercress, pineapple, and egg are all rich in vitamin B2, which plays an important role in good skin and coat condition.

Salmon oil is a good ingredient for skin and coat condition thanks to its omega-3 fatty acids.

If your dog is itchy, it may be because he is finding plant matter in the diet hard to digest. If you feel this could apply to the diet you are offering, cut back on the fruit and vegetable puree.

Sometimes chicken can be high in sodium, and this can result in itchiness. Check your source of chicken, especially if feeding a lot, and try some from a different source. Use a wider range of protein sources in the diet to cut down on the overall chicken content.

22-   FEEDING PUPPIES

(By this I mean what raw food to feed to your puppy; the chapter title isn't strictly a suggestion to feed raw puppy to your dog.)

It is safe to switch your puppy to raw food even as soon as you bring him home from the breeder at eight weeks of age. In fact, some breeders are beginning to wean puppies straight onto raw food, in which case your breeder will be full of encouragement and advice to help you continue this diet.

Normally, when you bring a new puppy home and wish to change his commercial food to a different brand, you should do so gradually. This is not necessary with raw food. You can stop the commercial diet immediately and start feeding complete raw meals. This actually keeps things simpler for the digestive system, rather than trying to mix dry/processed commercial food with fresh raw food.

Start in a similar way to how you would start an adult dog – a single protein source, in the form of chicken.

You can feed bone-in chicken to a puppy. Soft chicken bones should be absolutely manageable, and will be of great comfort when he starts teething. If you are nervous about feeding bones to a small puppy, feed ground meat with ground bone in it – but there is no need to worry about feeding whole bones. A raw-feeding breeder should have introduced chicken wings, carcass etc. to a puppy when it is only 3-4 weeks old.

Keep the bone content high for the first few days, then work toward the 10% bone ratio by feeding boneless chicken mince along with the bone-in chicken.

After a week on this, start adding other protein sources. Green tripe is a good thing to be adding soon. Leave a few days between each new protein source you add. Start mixing a teaspoon of vegetable/fruit puree with the meat, an occasional egg, oils and other supplements (see 'OTHER SUPPLEMENTS').

After a few weeks, start adding offal in small quantities, working up to the 10%-of-overall-diet ratio.

When your puppy's adult teeth begin erupting around 10-12 weeks of age, he will appreciate having harder bones to soothe the teething pain. Try some meaty lamb ribs, removing when he has had enough bone.

HOW MUCH TO FEED A PUPPY

Up until your puppy is four months of age, feed 5% - 8% of his total bodyweight (not adult bodyweight!) each day spread over four meals.

When he is between 4-6 months of age, feed 5%-8% but spread over three meals.

From 6 months to 1 year of age, the 5%-8% should be split over two meals.

At a year of age, he can be moved to adult portions (see chapter 'HOW MUCH TO FEED').

What to feed in the 5%-8% range depends on the size of your dog's breed. Smaller breeds normally need more than big breeds. So if your puppy is of a small breed, feed closer to the 8% mark; large-breed puppies should be fed closer to the 5% proportion of total bodyweight.

23- SUMMING UP

We should now have all the knowledge we need to get under way with feeding a healthy, safe and enjoyable raw-food diet. Let's recap some of the main points.

SAFETY

- We must never feed cooked bones.
- Fish must be frozen for at least a week before feeding.
- When choosing raw meaty bones to feed, we verge on the large side to reduce the chance of our dog attempting to gulp down big bone chunks.
- We understand how to defrost food safely to reduce bacteria forming on it (in the fridge, or small cuts in warm water).
- We know we must supervise our dogs when they are eating.
- We don't hesitate to contact our vets if we have any concerns for our dogs' health and wellbeing.

PRACTICALITIES

- We know we need to be a bit canny when it comes to sourcing our meat – especially to do so economically. Specialist online raw-food suppliers are becoming more common, and we should be able to find what we need there if none are available locally.

FEEDING

- We understand the benefits of both whole-prey and BARF model diets, and incorporate both benefits for our dogs.
- The backbone of balancing a diet is the ratio: 80% meat, 10% offal, 10% bone.
- We know that varying protein sources and other ingredients such as fruit and vegetables is key to a healthy diet.
- We are aware of 'superfoods' such as green tripe and salmon oil, and incorporate these in our dogs' diets.
- We remember that sometimes dogs may lose their appetite for a day and have a fast day, which mimics the behaviour of their wild ancestors.

MONITORING

- We keep an eye on our dogs' poo and respond appropriately with dietary adjustments.
- However, we remember to try and not get too obsessed with our dogs' poo. They are on a varied diet, so their poo will also be varied. The day after feeding raw meaty bones, poo will be hard and white; the day after feeding offal, it will be dark and soft. Only if we see the same sort of poo consistently should we look to make adaptations.

PERSISTING

- We know that dogs can be fussy eaters, and we should not give up if they don't immediately take to their raw diets (see 'HOW TO START').
- However, we also remember that we are doing this for our dogs' enjoyment as well as their health, and in the unlikely event that they simply can't get a taste for their delicious raw food, we should look for alternative diets.

I hope this guide to raw feeding has proven useful. Here are some suggestions for further reading on the subject of raw food for dogs:

'Give Your Dog a Bone', Dr Ian Billinghurst.

'Canine Nutrigenomics - The New Science Of Feeding Your Dog For Optimum Health', W. Jean Dodds and Diana R. Laverdue.

'Heal Your Dog the Natural Way', Richard Allport.

'Dog Health and Nutrition for Dummies', M. Christine Zink.